BEHOLDING

Donna Rose

Publisher Information

EBook Bakery

www.ebookbakery.com

email: dmrose21@cox.net

ISBN 978-1-938517-80-8

© 2018 by Donna M. Rose

Dedication

To my darling son, Étienne (Steven) Manuel Rose, who passed away at a very early age of eleven in the year nineteen hundred and ninety-one. Because of him I started writing poems, healing myself for the most tragic loss of my life.

My lovely daughter Cindy Marie Rose who I am ever so grateful for all the long hours of conversation we have shared over the years and for her guidance on many levels that has helped me understand life and all it has to offer.

To my soul mate for without meeting him over 50 years that passed us by I am sure I would have never been able to go deep within my heart and soul to experience the most beautiful feelings one knows when you truly love from the heart.

Since the loss of my mother and son, my heart had been closed. He had admired me in high school and when we met 50 years later at our class reunion, I knew from the start my heart belonged to him. He was very instrumental in channeling all that I received from him through the universal forces to be able to express it all in poems for others to read and grow from their own experiences. I will forever be thankful to him and I hope he has been rewarded through my wisdom to share my feelings and knowledge of love, life, losses and the process of healing one's self on paper. I know I have enhanced his life in a most unusual way as he has mine. Being in his presence whether near or far, we are solely connected to each other in such a beautiful way that I know no one can break the thread between us. "One Love for a Lifetime"

Steven Rose, Christmas 1987

The Poems

COSMIC ENERGY

ALWAYS NEAR

To know you are near even when you aren't
To know I can fly into your loving grace
and be captured in your magnificent embrace
even when you are not near
To know you hold me gently in your heart
Protecting me always
Calming my spirit when it is unsettled
I can spread my wings and fly with the Angels
to your loving grace
I am truly blessed and know you are always by my side
Life has such a beautiful way of keeping our dreams alive
Everything to me is what you are
You are life in a rainbow
of colors always shining through
Making every day a day of happiness
Life is such a beautiful wonder
Although your thoughts are held in your heart
I hear them whenever I look into those enchanting soothing eyes
I feel the everlasting embrace of your arms around me
even when you are not near
You have given me hope for a new day
We have given each other love our way
You take me to a place of peace and happiness
All I have to do is hold onto those thoughts of you
Your presence is always with me
even when you are not near
Loving you and you loving me is
Why we are here

ALWAYS

Follow me, here I am
Sitting right beside you
Holding your hand
Tender is the touch
Sifting through the tall grassy fields
Laughing delightfully so
Thought I lost you
You are back once again
Different, so different this time
Know this is what was intended for us
Waltzing, there's a magical feeling surrounding us
Love has a way all its' own
The clouds are smiling with us
The rain still warms our hearts
We both trusted and believed

ANOTHER PLACE IN TIME

Watching raindrops splash in puddles
Making their own water moving through the streams
The covered rocks sparkle with delight
As they are washed by the falling raindrops
They make rippling circles that float amongst the stars
The glow from the stars, make sparkles
like that of a kaleidoscope
You are placed in a world where all is aglow
Colors of all kinds softly lift you to a beautiful paradise
of what mankind has not been able to touch
You are swimming in the midst of colors
Adrift above the clouds you move so mysteriously free
What a wondrous day to live amongst the stars
The clouds wrap their clothing around your being
Untouched by the earth
You are warmed by the heavenly universe
Listen while the harp is being played by the Cherubs
The Dove slowly peacefully flies by
Giving peace to all who understand
Living among the stars
The piano keys make a melody of watery music
Bringing tears of joy to the soul
To know, to love, to live
Within another place in time

Destiny Amongst The Stars

Thinking of you
Trusting the universal forces
that brought us together

Listening to the sounds that surround us
Opening a field of joyous feelings of delightful music

Surrounds me with your everlasting love
I give of myself to only you
From the moment of time
We were destined to be together
Our souls just needed time to catch the wind
The wind blew our way
We soared like that of the hawk
Taking flight without a thought
Spreading its' wings ever so beautifully comforting us

We were destined to be together
The universal force gave us a galaxy to follow
We live amongst the highest lighted highway
Most of all we live for each other

We have been blessed by the grace of Mother Earth
She is the purest of Angels to live amongst the Stars
We will always be guided
And will return to the nest when it is right

For now, we live for today and love always

GIFTED

You were given a gift to use it wisely
You see yourself belonging to a higher place
Soaring through the universe while your
feet are still grounded
The awakening of your spiritual spirit
To know what life has bestowed upon you
The ability to live amongst the stars
To fly like our feathered friends
Symbolically with nature
Many days over he has given you lessons
Using your creative energies
Awakening the kundalini within
Seeing the visions while in meditation
Feeling the presence of many who surround you
Swirling like a musical top spins its energy
Knowing the Temperance within
The messenger of the Gods
Patience of what life will offer
The message will enhance the ability to
move through the wild with elegance
with knowledge, peace and love
Understanding and Patience
A gift of many virtues
Spread your wings and let the
Feathered friend guide you

HARMONY OF SOULS

I lay with your body resting upon mine
Your touch is very sensual
You know just where to caress my body
Slowly smoothing the layers of the silken skin
Moving to an area that feels beautiful to the two
The rapture is always new
Like the day at dawn
Or the night at dusk

You never fail to excite me
Arousing the inner love that holds the heart
Peaceful joy surrounds us
We are lighted by our souls
That gives warmth to every touch

So close, oh so very close are we
In the harmony of our souls

HENCE YOU CAME

Don't look too far over the meadows
The future has been paved for all
Journeys you travel are planned before your time
Walk the mile, venture lightly
Look beyond the horizon and the stars
See the air caress the winds
Chiming with the endless tides
Know that you are in good hands, always
You came from the womb of a precious being
Know you belong to only Him
As the water creates its' path
And as it flows, it carries the wind with it
Yes, today's life fell unto thee

INSPIRATIONAL LOVE

You inspired me to move with the flow of motion
To follow my dreams, they will carry me to a distant land
I am loved you are always there for me
I may not see you in the flesh, but feel you ever so
I close my eyes and feel your presence
Touching me, comforting my soul
Listening when others ears were closed
Gazed upon my being like no other
Brought me peace and love
I gave you the same
Through the universe we see and touch each other
The closeness we have is only known by two
Destiny has carried us over centuries
Move, move gently with me
Take my hand let me comfort you in your need
Never to leave your side – move with me
Together, side by side

LISTENING TO COLORS

Sounds of colors falling on the parchment
Enchanting words are heard
Listen
The words are tiptoeing across the parchment
Now smiling at me
Makes me feel wonderful
Such happiness you can feel from them
They are dancing now
Like a ballerina
When she moves the colors turn different shapes
The shapes tell a story of her life
She is smiling so brightly
Twirling brings out the shapes of the colors
You see them through the wide spread of her wings
You can feel her lightness all around you
Listen, as she shows herself
Shaping into this magnificent sound of happiness
Listen, you can tell her story
She just winked at me

LOOKING GLASS

What is it you see?
I know not for it sees me
I seem to be in a bubble floating through air
Carrying me over mountains and oceans
Rivers streaming by as the wispy wind captures my eyes
A glow of sunshine caressing my heart
The weeping willow tree not knowing how to stop
What is it you see?
I know not for it sees me

LOST

I lay in wake, you are there in spirit
I wake in morning you are there within my soul
See you not, touch you not.
Gone from touch and sight
I cry, overwhelmed by your loss
Though I look for you – thought I saw you passing by
Cried, you not – lost so lost
When I opened my heart, I never held back
I love sincerely as I care whole-heartedly unconditionally
You have been an important person from years past
The bleakness that hovers over my soul is heavy now
Like that of wet snow
I know not when it will lift
I walk in silence and no comfort do I find
I cry and cry and when I smile it is unwilling
Helplessly lost in the unsettled emotions that lie within
Will we ever see each other again? I fear not.
So unbearably sad I want to run....to where?....I don't know
Anywhere where I can find comfort

Past and Present

Capturing years past through shadows of light
Passing each other of years miles away
Close friends like a caterpillar is to a butterfly
We created our own heaven through time
You held my hand and I yours
We shared all our emotions and knew the heart
Distance never distant us
As the souls traveled through endless years
We found each other once again
Connecting again under stars
Moments shared in silence, our presence wrapped in silk
Capturing our inner souls we moved to another tune
Separating never – Bonded again through our souls
Cherished love of purist friendship of years ago
Always there for each other with such compassion and love
We lived under our own creation
While the fluttering wings of the Angelic presence
held us together to nurture and grow in the harmony of
her light
Once again – given of ourselves to life
Sharing sacred moments for our hearts only
Comforting the soul always by just being there
Protecting all we hold precious for each other
Never letting go

PRICELESS

Definitive happiness in our shell
Whispers a soft radiant smell
Warms us when the night is cool
Comfort comes in thoughts of new
Stepping out when all is safe
Looking down upon our fate
We see the world when they cannot
Above the heavenly cotton tops
What wondrous joy that we possess
Traveling from the earthly nest
To find our hearts upon his breast

Rhythmic Moves

The trees hold the water
You hold the tears
Together you can let them flow
Across the ocean seas

The Swan moves effortlessly
Above the waters and through the skies
Charming our ever open space of views

Within yourself to always be present
With all you know and do
Carrying yourself above the morning dew

Smile at the life that has been given unto you
Move with the flow of energy as sensuously as you do
The movements of your body tell an unusual story
Moving to the rhythm of the castanets
Your hips sway back and forth in a rhythmic move
The sounds from the Spanish guitar creates the spinning and the twirls
You create the moves and you know how it feels to be loved
You glow while your eyes dance with the stars
and rest upon your every step

Let the trees hold the water
You no longer need to hold the tears
You have found yourself once again
In the rhythm of music and love

SOMEPLACE IN TIME

Soft moving tides that sweetly glided through the
laughter of joy that nestled within the spirit
moved gently into the open space like the colors
of the rainbow sweeping the endless sky
Thought of you
Joyous smiles seeped through the uncovered flesh
Spring opened a window of pleasure
What wondrous feelings we possess and pass to one another
Through the universe we are bond
Within the winds of tides, heard you thought of me
My heart smiled

SPACE - EVER LOVING SPACE

Here I am – haven't gone anywhere
You – are where?
Tides are rushing in seeping through the flow of emotions
Feeling comfort as they move in and out
Waters are warm and calm
The storm has moved on
Can you hear me?
Words of unspoken love – listen
Listen to the raindrops playing our song
They gently caress the piano keys
Moving gracefully over each key
Creating an artistry of love
With the wind blowing on the cello
The storm has passed
Do you see me?
Waters are warm and calm
I am basking in the stillness found in you
Your presence warm – soothing the flesh over me
Flowing – flowing with the moving air of peace
Here I am – haven't gone anywhere

THE CONNECTION

She knew not what she read
Each line sent a chill through her body
She continues to read for the unknown was intriguing - blissful
Bringing knowledge and wisdom
She didn't choose this path
She was taken there
I watched as the words danced across the paper in song
What the author brings is extravagantly unwinding
She continued to read and the chill continued to engulf
her innocent soul
When she finished reading
The look upon her face was truly amazing
The connection without words spoken was evident to the two
The silence of thought captured them

THE PIANO KEYS

My fingers are moving to the piano man
They are gliding over the keys with a mind of their own
Each note played is ecstasy in ecstasy
I love the way each note turns over and over again

Catching every breath you take and throwing it to the wind
The wind takes it and blows it over the horizon
The water circles them and folds them in and out of the waves
They move so pleasantly over the waters

The tune changed and you are gliding in a different world
Knowing life pours out of the keys
Is part of your life moving with the tides of your inner being
Keeping you alive – you bask in the open fields of joy

You are floating and the wind lifts up your wings
How beautiful is the other side that you have privilege to see
All that you had thought was lost is never to be
There with you always they will be
Sing, sing joyously over the keys and float on heavens knees
Smile for loving all is all you can be

THE SPIRIT OF THE DEAD WATCHING OVER YOU

Espirito de Morte me vé por mi
It flashes through your body
Like the wind trailing behind the storm
Out of nowhere your body is filled with this uncontrollable feeling of fear
Sporadically your thoughts create your body to have uncontrollable
waves of awareness driven by this rush
Your mind travels far beyond this plane
There is no shape or size as it folds in and out of your body
It paralyzes you, frightens you, you become breathless a victim to the rush
It hangs over you and all you see is this gray heavy misty cloud
hovering over you while you are unable to move
Slowly you begin to breathe
You are free of this frozen state
It brings understanding to life
It leaves you shivering and you are one with many others
Over the years you understand this darkness and are able to
work with the unknown
Traveled roads are forever long

TRAVELING JUST TRAVELING

The roads are endless and the destination is where...
I am free and my wings take me above and beyond
Floating with the rhythm of time
This is marvelous and so enchanting
I meet no one yet everyone surrounds me
Floating in time
The waves of my journey are spectacular
I see colors of many shapes and they talk to me
A rhapsody of music embraces my heart
I am full of life and life full of me
The ears listen and the eyes see with such intensity
Smiles come and go and the wonders of my travels are exhilarating
My feet are moving yet going nowhere
The wondrous ecstasy of love is you
You are the one who catches your heart
When you send out your bow it captures another's soul
You move again with the wind
Your beautiful wings are widespread in an endlessly motion of truth
bringing the presence of your soulmate in full view
We are life - we are love - we smile with the love that glows
Through our spirit it captures something so everlastingly beautiful
Traveling, just traveling together in time
Gliding so effortlessly we are there...

WADE IN THE WATER

I am a ripple in this vast ocean of lands
A feather in the air floating gracefully until I land
Carrying no cares
Only my love for you always

I'm the breath you take every day
You're my life because you hold me so dear

Your sweet kind ever caring heart
Carries mine within the folds of yours

I know you, you know me
We have lived many years ago
Those years were part of our souls finding each other
Learning of each other until we meet again

I'm the teardrop that never cried
The joy of life bringing love to your side
I'm the smile that brightens your day
The sleep that always comes our way

You're the joy that comes into my heart
the moment I lay my eyes on you

You're the love that shines through and through
glowing through the night to keep our love alive

As I wait for your return
I am the wave in the water wading in the wet sand

What I Bring To Thee

A warm tender heart that stretches beyond the silken walls
Pure and delightful
Always there for you
The joy of knowing you are loved
Giving and knowing the receiver smiles with delight
Trusting to be able to let your feelings move
With the warmness of the other joys that fill the heart
Waves of journeys have floated you above the earth
The heart gives out so many sounds
You have been captured on its' journey of musical notes
Trust for you are always protected
I am here for you
Like the endless tides we move together
We have life to offer to each other
We have lived for this moment
You fed me delightful memories
Time to bring them to light
I am here for you
Know you are here for me
Our hearts are on a spiritual wave of tides
Open the joy and live
Let love comfort you
Bring you back to the Heart of tenderness
I am here for you – trust me
Relax in the arms of one who cares

ÉTIENNE

ANGEL OF RESCUE

Her mind busy with thoughts, covered by fear
While her soul, hungered for the love of her last born

Cherished memories touched her heart through
the softness of a winged friend
As her loved one swiftly moves from one passageway to another
She buried her soul in sadness
Only to be awakened by the sweet tenderness of a familiar voice

Overhead a sky of gray silk covered the pure white clouds of yesterday
and her eyes rested lightly upon a silhouette of the love she once knew

With a single thought she embraced the child
Each step feather light, in the silence the heart stood still

His life no longer His
Hers no longer Hers
Swept away by the sweet angelic music calling from afar
The Angel looks on; for darkness holds no fear

Her busy mind and bewildered heart covered
with layers of
Why???
She moves on......
His Life begins.....

A Very Special Place

Let's spend the day together, tomorrow or the next
Hoping for a clear day to pass our way
As the sun shines brightly upon your face
The meadows bloom in the morning light
Ah! Ecstasy, the pleasure of us together
That "Special Place" where now I rest
Walking through the marshlands, across the slopes we go
The chilling frost upon our noses
Imagine only you and me upon this earthly plane
A place of peace, a place of grace
Oh! that very "Special Place"
Where our hearts became as one, our hands held tight,
Yes, I remember that day of joy and laughter as you
opened your heart to mine
And in the days to follow, I will follow close behind

COMFORT ME

You have touched my heart in many ways,
I have not gone, just in another place
My travels for now are vast and far
Yet in my heart you will stay

Let not this day depart us none
You my child knows Gods Will, be done

So carry on each day in time
Remembering what we had
And what shall be

You are my dearest love
And I am here for you with open arms
To shield, comfort, and guide your steps
For I have not gone, just in another place to watch over thee

FEELING GOOD ABOUT MYSELF

I'm not a Nerd
I'm just as happy as a flea
Please don't put those silly clothes on me
A shirt and tie, polished shoes, Oh No!!! knee highs
We must not forget the jacket and vest
And of course the nicely pressed pants
Who is this Dude? 'Tis not I, I want to be a little guy
Mommy sometimes doesn't understand that little guy,
whom I am
Yet as I recall, dressed to beat the band
I smiled as I looked at my reflection in the mirror
Man, I looked so grand
Charcoal gray jeans, crisp white ironed shirt
Topping it off with red tie and suspenders
Shy as I may have been, stylish loafers swept my feet
And with all of this, my heart began to beat
Left foot, right foot, I began to move
Sliding across the floor, like a lady sweeping with her broom
I danced for my mother
Entertainment, entertainment for all to see and what but not to enjoy me
I looked at my mother then she winked her eye
I danced until I saw that smile and heavenly glow in her sparkling green eyes
The memory would stay with us for more than a day
I knew I would always be her "Little Sweetheart" in every way
Yes, Feeling Good About Myself, letting me be me
And of course, you would never guess
I put those silly clothes on me
Feeling good about myself, letting me be me
Although I fuss with all my might, secretly I loved the sight
Of all those silly clothes on me
Thanks Mom

Forgotten Not

In the loneliness of night, bewildered by darkness
No one holds me tenderly, no one keeps my heart
When the morning mist appears, the birds begin to sing
The brightness of day lightens our way
Do you miss thee?
When I hold a buttercup under my chin, I remember your smile once again
I walk up the stairs and look within
Your face is everywhere, your presence never far
The voice so very clear
Do you miss thee?
You blessed my heart with ecstasy untold and filled my heart with joy
The Virgin who watches over us
And Cupid with his bow
My days are filled with memories of past and old
You my Love I will never forget
But miss you ever so

I WILL ALWAYS BE

Do not be afraid, I am with you
I will hold your hand all the way

You have been my Rock
You are in my Heart
I love you and I am free

Do not let the tears overwhelm you
Let your emotions seep through your pores
Look around the corner, I am with you
Light and love will show the way

I know you can endure
I know you will explore
I love you and I am free

Keep the fires burning within you
Let the souls become as one

Then I will be your rock and me within your heart
I love you and I am safe

IF YOU WERE A DREAM

If you were a Dream
I'd marvel at Dreams, which have come to me
You would be that Angel who I often see
The Kitten I love to squeeze
Those last blooming Flowers at the end of fall
Or maybe the Weeping Willow Tree who hides from us all
When winter makes its first full break
The darkness of the day, which comes too soon
The early morning snowflakes caressing our gloom
My mind at its' highest peak
My soul while it travels when I sleep
If you were a Dream
All these wonderful things, you would be
I'd let no one ever take this Dream from me

IMAGES

If I had not known your Heaven, I would not know where you are
For in the bleakness of nights she came with your message from afar
The feeling of your presence so near
A ray of light, the day so bright
The meadows how they blossomed, with the sweet fresh smell of spring
Butterflies flew swiftly by
Oh the joys of nature, bring so many memories to the eyes
The cold blistering day of winter
The snowflake that lost its' way
In the early morning hours, I heard you call my name
Across the endless ocean
Beyond my wildest dreams
I think of you in Heaven, she expressed what she had seen
The beginning of spring – her Heaven
The meadows, the flowers, the colors soft and bright
She showed me a picture, we spoke of you that night
I spoke of the ocean and the peacefulness that you knew
As we sat in precious silence, our hearts began to sing
We felt the joy of living, the music that you bring
Oh! The beautiful thought of Heaven
With the season's nature brings
The peaceful warmth of sunlight, the beauty of a stream
The snowflake that lost its' way
Found his Heaven in a dream
Oh God, do we all not know our Heaven
The peacefulness of spring, the bright sunlight in the meadows
The cold that winter brings, the turning of the trees in fall
The calmness of the ocean walls
Nature in full flight
Be it divine to know our Heaven
Then peace will come with night

IN TIME

I walk in utter silence
The day becomes the night
I lost my way to shyness
I lost all of my sight
I feel the early morning dew resting sweetly on my lips
I wander through the forest, the trees become my friends
My refuge, my pretend
Oh! How I long to find me again
Not the perils of my life
No longer would I wonder if you were in my sight
Although I live in disbelief of that painful, stricken day
My heart still heavily burden on why you left that way
In the years to follow, my friend you will always be
My light, my love, my happiness, my "Angel come to be"
No longer will I wonder
For in my heart I'll find, closeness of our love
That very special bond in time

KNOWING

If I had not known your Heaven
I'd know not where you are
In the dismal days ahead
You'll come from afar
The light has shown for you, my dear
One day it will shine for me
I could search the oceans, lands and universe
I could search far beyond what my eyes can see
Your Heaven is a peaceful place
Safe for you, one day for me

Looking Within

There was a man that once I knew
Who saw your problems through and through
Had I given him the chance
Would you still be standing here with me?
Enjoying all the times we use to share and know
Time for love, laughter and time to understand and grow
How I wish my heart had been opened
To hear the cry of the soul in need
To have seen the light that was shining through
To have listened to the man
His deepest thoughts were of you
He looked within to understand what he knew?
He knew what you were seeking through and through
You might have just opened your heart to me
Given me a chance to see you through
The days, weeks and months you crumbled inside the womb
Would not have been if I had known
The sadness you carried all day long

MYSTERIOUSLY FREE

If I could look into your little mind
Go beyond the folds of time
What would the imagination bring?
I imagine many things
Soft notes that the piano sings
Humming from the guitar strings
The joy which made your face aglow
A smile on your lips only you would know
A twinkle in your eyes
The tears that you cried
Thoughts you thought
Things you've seen
The mystery of the mind holds so many things
Like the calmness of the ocean breeze
Blowing the leaves around the trees
It's the mountains high above
It's the silver lining in the clouds of love
A fresh breath of air to fill our lungs
Never far, always near
I'd take that gusty wind to blow your troubles into the sea
Then the mind would flow
Mysteriously Free

Out of the Womb

You came to me on a whispered wing
Sought your world and so many things
Your place on earth was not for long
Missions here were for a loved one
Gifted you were and a gift to me
For the love you taught was timeless energy
Once we saw, again we shall see
For the Angels came to take care of thee
Your presence here was short to be
I saw that in the glow of thee
I knew you well, as you knew me
Until the whispered wing came to set you free
Time shared, time given, all you taught, all you knew
Left millions of people under the rainbow
Without a view

Rebirth

Do not go to my graveside and weep
I have not died, I only sleep
When you see the sun appear
Be very still look around, for I am near

I was here to teach so many things
To give you love, joy, peace; and all the wonders nurturing brings
'Twas not my love all that was needed?
I know now for I had to fly far beyond the heavenly skies
Though the physical person no longer in site, my energy is warm and bright
There to always guide you
There to always walk beside you
There to listen when no one seems to care
A shoulder to cry on and bury the tears
Through the clearest of skies our laughter shines bright
Even in the darkest of nights
I have not gone so much to make a place for you
For dying is only letting go of the old and the beginning of a new
So don't look so sad, bewildered or alone
Like the lioness who never leaves her cubs,
yet they go astray
I have many roads to travel today
But tomorrow, tomorrow I'll find my way back to you to stay

SADNESS

Who am I?
What do you see?
I turn my eyes from you, you turn yours from me
I dare not look again for fear of what you'll find
You care too much as I watch you look within
I run from your gaze like a fire in full blaze
Still, so very still the air
Silence, ever so silent
An Angel hums an Angelic song
Fear, no thought, just fear I feel
I know where you are, I hold my breath
Slowly I come upon you
I cry out
"Oh God, what have you done to me?"
I freeze, I shake, take you from that horrible fate
I know now what we two tried so painfully to hide
The sadness we both felt deep inside
You, knowing more that I,
I cry out "Oh God, why, why, why?"

SEARCHING

My Angel, my Sweetheart, close to my bosom you slept
Watched your first smile press through those little thin lips
Tears, you knew not what they were
Every minute of the day was filled with laughter and cheer
I closed my eyes and turned around
What you once felt was nowhere around
You were gone
I've searched the ocean, the playground, and my heart
Remembering our little hideaways
I roamed
Do you not see the candle light at night?
I know where your are, beyond my reach and not in sight
My heart cries out, how I long to see
Dreams, dreams of you so near
Smiling, playing, calling my name
Do you really see me?
I'm over here, never far, always near
Searching my heart, my mind and soul
This is not good-bye
I know you wait for me
Somewhere on the other side

SERENITY

Watching a Rose blossom in early spring
The beautiful soft colors nature brings
To hold a pebble in your hand
A ray of sunlight on your face
To look far beyond the Rainbow
God's heaven – our resting place
The mystery of life will always be
So as we watched the Rose bloom in early spring
We also watched the pebbles fall
The warmest memories and precious joys
was having you as our little boy
The colors of the Rainbow glowed far beyond
The light which charmed your heart to the open arms
Your Paradise, Your Heaven, God's home
Our love for you will always carry a special bond
Our hearts our light and our love forever strong
For us, you are not gone
You just traveled far beyond

SHADOWS

I look behind me
Are you there?
I see nothing
Where has it gone?
I know I felt you near and saw
My eyes blink, my heart cries
Traveling, endlessly amidst the stars
Gliding heavenly, peacefully
Soaring through the universe
Watching over me
Yes, yes, there it is again, but I don't see
Feel, yes, I feel you all around me
As I smile within, my heart is warm
My Shadow, no, yours, I came to know
For in my heart you have nestled
This Darling is where you belong

THE MESSAGE

I lay in restless sleep
In the stillness of the night
My subconscious opens my mind to new light
My soul leaves my body and travels far beyond
Floating, floating, I know not where I'm going
Ringing of the telephone, yet there's no one there
Knocking on the door, no one, nowhere
Night turns to day, the day turns to night
I fall asleep again, the ringing loud and clear
What has happened? What is going on?
Do I imagine? Is this beyond?
Like the bird outside my window, the Robin came to me
Trying to guide me through the universal mystery
A message, a message, a message for me
Meditate, pray
He's trying to reach you, let him through
The softness of his hand, resting on my thigh
Shakes me in the night to say "Hi Mom, it's me, Étienne"
A warning, an opening of the eyes
Days pass, the message is inside
I stumble through the days, clouds still blind my eyes
What I saw, I did not see, until she screamed at me
The message so clear and true, could only come from
a Love one such as you

THE QUARTZ CRYSTAL

Although you left in such a way
An accident, an accident, I told myself each day
As the days move slowly by
I often wonder what you've seen
To understand nature's plan
To know yourself much more than I
'Tis the wisdom only you possessed
in order to travel to the other side
As I look into the looking glass, I see the days,
which have past us by
While the stone shines brightly before my eyes
The stone to me was just a beautiful sight
To you, my Darling, it held
Eternal Light
You loved to hold it in your hands
The awareness of your heart and the depths of your mind
was far beyond this place in time
The stone possessed a greater strength,
which you felt but could not explain
If I knew then, what I know now
that precious beautiful healing stone
Would have been yours to own

WAITING PATIENTLY

I'm not quite sure just how it happened or how it came to be
I found myself in a very different place, one that frightened me
Faces I never saw before, yet those I came to love and adore
They watched me, cared for me and tried to understand
Not so trusting, frightened and bewildered, I showed another side of me
Time flew by and the days grew long, there were only two faces I longed to see
In the mist of the evening, my heart skipped a beat
Oh God, those two beautiful faces were resting at my feet
Oh how my heart beat, unable to speak, that very special moment I held long
She gave me a "hello", a kiss and a hug
I embraced her, the same because of our love
The second "hello" held a part of her heart in her hands
and as we touched, I felt loved again
Oh Wow! Oh My! Is that for me?
Yes my Little Darling it's called "The Giving Tree"
We sat there in silence as she began to read,
and the sweetness of her voice set my mind at ease
Intensely we listened to the ringing of her words,
singing through the pages bringing
new meaning and light into our hearts that night
Many days have passed, months and almost a year
I've called you and ran past
But you were overwhelmed with fear
Remember how I sat "Waiting Patiently"
listening to the ringing of your beautiful voice
as you read to me
Please open your heart and let me through
I'm "Waiting Patiently" just for you
When I come again, silent as it may be
Open up your heart and welcome me
For you see, I can only rest, once I know how much you love thee

YESTERDAY

If we could bring back yesterday
What would we change today?
To understand why yesterday was
We must know why today is
Tomorrow will follow today
Why? 'Because it's just the way it is'

Does that explain the uncertainty of today?
Only that yesterday passed and today is today
To learn from yesterday,
Is to know why today is today and tomorrow will
flourish a better way

We did not know what yesterday would be
Confused, sad, bewildered we've seen
The most precious part of our life taken from our dreams
Our dreams became our sadness, our light became our darkness

Where is the laughter which used to crowd our hearts?
Like the bursting of the dam the tears flooded our hearts
We bow our heads in sadness, our bodies slumped in pain
We still know not why Yesterday has come about this way
We only know today
Yesterday happened
Tomorrow we can change

HEALING FROM LOSS

Comfort of Silence

It can be peaceful without words heard
Or worry curled in a knot at the pit of your stomach
waiting to pour out of the lips
Sometimes it brings a sudden jog in a quiet way
It burns deep within the soul when one anticipates
the unspoken voice
You sit quietly and wait in the deep silence
Comfort found within the folds of silence wrapped around your being

Days of Time

Days are moving like the sea
Close your eyes and see more than you can touch
Where did it all go?
You walk the shoreline and let the water trickle through your toes
Soothing your feet while they sink into the wet sand
Thoughts float as the sea takes them back and forth
Recalling a happier time in life
Your heart smiles remembering when
What lies beyond today?
The hour glass is slowly draining
The day moves on
Your feet no longer walk
Sitting by the window the light burns across the way
Memories unfold as you gaze into nowhere
Thoughts take you to your special place
Rocking yourself in the comforts of your space
The day has ended

Embracing Loss

The body weeps crystal clear teardrops from within
Forming a surge of wet cleansing moisture around the tissues of the skin
You try to comfort yourself by holding onto that which is no longer there
Your body no longer upright – you quiver
Emotional sadness covers you with a blanket of shadows
You want to cry out – no one there to hear your cries
No longer in touch with the loss
You close your eyes and bring in the music of love
Love the only love of your life comforts you through the day
Though he is miles away
Through an energy only known by you
Away – yet not far from view
Eyes are upon you – hide from sight
You smile at the world and only you know the pain
Finding the beauty in the day
Brings you to a place you can hold onto
You move so gracefully and elegantly – no one knows your pain
Others only see the shell that covers you
You hold yourself with grace
You are the heart and soul of moisturized flesh weeping from within

EMOTIONS RUNNING WITH THOUGHTS

Forming in the subconscious
The cotton cushioned heart absorbs the sweltering flesh
Mastering the unknown of flowing thoughts
Bringing those moments and words to life again
Muddling through the verse of phrases formed by words untouched
Feelings of rushing winds whipping around the thoughts
Running, running and running again
The body is still of movement
The mind races around and around moving nowhere
Conversations move in and out of the thoughtless mind
Endlessly there is no end, the heart throbs
The outcome awaits the conclusion
For the mind cannot help the rush of emotions
The emotions linger in the heavy heart, waiting

FEATHER LIGHT

Knowing your heart was captured
You lived in a place of pure delight
Knowing nothing lasts forever
You became lost in the flow of emotions
Drifting from one memory to another

When your heart opened it was seeing a rose bloom for the first time
Extraordinary grace gave way to the flowering bud
which held the joy of life
With the morning dew dripping from the velvety petals
Wrapped in the evergreen leaf for comfort

You saw your heart smoothing out the wrinkles
that had settled overnight
Days passed, the petals fell one by one
Months of understanding nature to love
Your petals fell too
Your heart became motionless
Your cares consumed
Your eyes lived in a solution of watery sorrow

Letting go was so much harder than saying "hello"
No one to rest your thoughts on
Your inner peace kept you whole
You moved to the music of the soul
Feeling the everlasting presence of the Angelic spirit
within the heart of souls

You move with ease as the gentle breeze sweeps you off your feet
They seem to capture the essence of dancing
Gliding over the surface never touching earth

IN FLIGHT

Where am I going?
Just take me away – anyplace
I seem to move nostalgically among the stars in the Universe
Traveling through the Milky Way
Sleep – precious sleep never comes
My body a vessel carrying months of sadness
Moving like a painters brush on canvas
Splashing colors on top of more colors of emotions
As they come to light, dimness shines through
Covering your heart while the heart sleeps
You're experiencing an out-of-body flight
Mirroring days past
Caught in a whirlwind of air
You continue to move in flight
Beautiful wings of white carry you
Universal waves comfort you on this journey
The night unfolds and morning comes to past
Life once again will bloom and your breast will blossom
You have traveled the earth many times over and the wings have
kept you safe and alive
That which is unseen slowly escapes you
when you decide to live again
Live with the fullest of life
Take a moment and Rest

INNER FEELINGS

Each day runs its' own path
Like running water, sometimes hot, then cold
Emotions are very similar with one thing different
You feel the pain gushing through your veins
Soothing water escapes the eyes, you smile
Sudden spouts of laughter ring out
You are not alone
The lonesome body doesn't feel that
You have been here before
The journey was long and sorrowful
Longing for the rising sun to bring warmth
You see yourself running to open arms of love
You only see – the emptiness smothers your dreams
You can't escape this – you have to work with it daily
You have been here before
The journey was long and sorrowful
Emotions take over your being
Let it out – let it out
Don't hold back
Tears will fall when they may
Let them fall
You have been here before
The journey was long and sorrowful
When all the sorrow has dried out
You will joyously smile a celebration
You have loved and not ashamed of your feelings
You will love again and again – smile

Pure Essence

The air is sweet and calming to her soul
She moves to the gentle waves of the oceans
Love has managed to stay with her
As she basks in the days ahead
Knowing her heart is a bloom again

She can hold the beauty of life
Knowing she never shadowed her dreams
Living the moments as fruitfully as she may

The glow that permeates from her being
Is captured in a whimsical breath of air
What she holds dear is a gift to all who dare
to fall under her gaze

When she moves the body smiles at you
There are no boundaries for her offerings
Always there to pleasure the day
For the heart is pure

SERENITY OF MEMORIES

Quietly sitting in the morning of the day
Thoughts of you spray my heart – gently - softly
The aura in my dwelling permeates throughout under the
miraculous glow of candle light that only enhances all that surrounds me
Time washes away all the sorrow and opens a window of peace
Peace we respect for all our tomorrows
The wonders of life begin once again with love
Moments will always come and go
Like the whispers that move gently through the wispy leaves of a Willow tree
To hold those moments close to your heart comforts the soul and soothes the mind
Knowing that life has only one beginning and one end
Will dictate what those moments hold for you and how you move with them...

Silence of the Soul

It settles inside your body and slowly encompasses your being
You become motionless and confused
The silence is unbearable and you move through the midst of it all
Your thoughts evolve endlessly like that of a spinning top
The unknown to you is the darkest of night
Untouched by words not heard
The resolution has no end and you ponder away
Moving gracefully with the unknown and sadly you lay in a cocoon
Spring brings colors beautifully sad to the heart
Summer warmth cools the soul
Quiet yourself to the sadness and all that surrounds you
The loss once again is a mystery

SLOWLY MOVING

You wonder when it would start to move
The flow of emotions begins at many levels
The first was the seed of sadness and your mind and heart held joy not
Somehow anger stepped in and your world became mercury of explosions
The ordinary things you walk through daily became a jungle
Feeling you had made it over the dam you settled in with the flow of water
Morning came and you felt calm but something was unexplainable painful
Unforeseen by human eyes you managed to move with the unbalanced flow of air
Slowly, not knowing, it engulfed your heart and the river of emotions
pushed their way through the tear stained heart
As the river passed by, you cried
Silently inside – overwhelming the heart – you held it all in
What you have grown to know doesn't comfort you now
The sorrow is like that of a vacuum surrounding your being
With eyes closed while you listen to the piano,
the keys have a mind of their own moving to the loneliness you feel
Taught by the greatest of all, you move to another world
All the present things that surround you are grey
You are lost in the swirling pain of loss
Time, precious time will wrap its' glow around you
Just give it time and let it move

STAGES

Sitting quietly while the movie is being played out
There are many parts to be filled
Watching the actors on stage
Beginning to understand what has just taken place
Like holding sand in the palms of your hands
Watching as it slowly disappears from its' holding place

Life stages evolving around your being
The colors of the actors coming to life
One stage of life after another

Walking the sands with such overwhelming sadness
Filling the empty heart
Years of healing brought you to a comfortable place

Slowly stepping into the earth again
Carefully choosing where you wanted to be
Angels' guidance all the way
Finding yourself on a plane where many
footprints have traveled

Opening the heart of a very wonderful sultry women
Entering waters unknown
Only to leave them behind

THE AWAKENING

Late in July I awoke in the early morning hours
To find my soul enriched with such beautiful energy

For months I traveled to an area nurturing my inner being
Angels were by my side all the way
I remember smiling as they touched my heart
Keeping me afloat and focused
Letting me take whatever steps I wanted to
Knowing I would soon see the horizon

My life was beginning all over again
My wings carried me over planes I had never been before
My heart never stopped playing the musical instruments that soothed the soul

Throughout the journey my heart and mind came to a warm understanding
of another being so dear to me, always
When I knew he would be safe and understand me
It was time to move beyond the circle
I stepped out and my feet moved gracefully
across the pavement as my wings were trying to keep up with me

I am just floating and floating to my rhythm of loving myself
Taking nothing for granted but holding on to what I can
When it is time to let the hands separate, you know

Still, I am smiling for life brought me to a very memorable place in time
That very special time will always be nestled in the cup of my heart

THE MESSENGER

I came to you from winds untold
Many years I've watched you grow and grow
In looking upon your present state
I knew it was time to make this date

You spoke of me to a friend
It was time to take that flight with a winged friend

Wisdom comes in many ways
That is why I came this day
To come in three's is most high a sign
For you can't get higher than the "Holy Trinity Divine"

I have listened to your call and you to mine
Now listen to your heart and you will find
The peace and joy we brought to mind

For in the end we all shall be
One with God and the Holy Trinity

THE MOORS

She walked the moors in the dismal early morn
Felt the heavy dew settle on her quivering lips
Tears trickled down her soft crescent cheeks and rested on her breast
The warmth of the dew softened her heart
Yet the pain within held her thoughts
She cried, no sounds to be heard
She reached out to touch nothing but the air
The rains came and drenched her sadden soul
Washing the early morning away
The sun will shine one day and brighten her heart
Until then she wanders the moors

THE STORM WITHIN

Knowing how to calm the storm is the means of happiness
By bringing it into the core of your being
Moving the waters over the waterfall
Gently soothing the soul that carries it all
The chalice of your life
Is life itself
Be with it all and smile
Love yourself let it permeate throughout your soul
The love from you will flow through the waters
Be well
Know you are the one in control
Let the storm blow through the fires
Find peace in the waterfall
Let your heart lead you and your mind will follow

Universal Truth's

What mysteries lie in the Universal Truth's?
Under the layers of the moving clouds
We connect to the other side through the universe and the cosmic energy
Seen not by the human eye but through the third eye
Heard not through the hollow drum that is connected to our head
But through the winds that carry the cosmic energy

The channeling of the tunnel holds much to be seen
The wind carries the whispers of love
The third eye carries the love of all
Through the spinning of the tornado that catches the flow of energy
Spitting it out at us like the light which comes from a shooting star
Honor that which you receive and use it wisely
Connecting you to all levels - you are the nucleus of attunement

Angels of the heavens and those on earth
Guide you on your journey in life
Hold fast to those truth's you receive
Honor and respect them giving new birth to those in need
Compassion, love and peace will guide you in helping others
in their quest to become whole again
Trust the Universe respect the Angels above and those on earth to heal you

UNSEEN

Somethings we never see, yet we know there is movement
With that movement a new day comes our way
Our bodies bask in the wake of it all

We listen from the little drum on the sides of our head
We see from the two glowing stones
Then you have the third eye that opens so much more

Our bodies listen and become engulfed with all that surrounds us
Creating a cavity to hold everything in it

As you gracefully move throughout the days
You find what is needed to continue to nurture your being
What isn't needed you gently let it fall back to mother earth

Emotions are the hardest to let go even if they no longer serve a purpose
We hold on and hold on and soon we have created an unhealthy being

Knowing when to leave the dust behind is vital to our growth
We go through life meeting many Masters given special guidance

Remembering the storm is only as strong as we allow it to be

The life we create is our own
From the creation we give birth to our spirit
The rain will always fall downward
The sun will always shine from above
The wind will blow in all directions

WHAT ABOUT ME?

You feel it coming and you have no control
Or do you?
It's like no other feeling
Unexplainable yet very powerful
You may suppress it over and over again
There is no escaping it
Then you know all too well what travels behind it
Quiet yourself and go within
Nurture yourself as no one else can
Know when it passes life will smile again
Until then work with it all
You are not alone in this battle
Many have come and gone
Trust your heart you will get through this
Continue to move like the wind under your footsteps
Comfort the soul and the soul will comfort you
It will move in its' own time
This you cannot force to happen
Everything in its' own time
Know the beauty in what was
Never lost, just tucked away
Love will smile on you another day

WONDERING

Your body moves with the ease of a cloud weaving in and around the universe
As the thoughts travel you see through the folds
Drifting through the splashing waves, we move
Traveling up and down hills, we breathe
Flowing through the gusty winds, we fly
Taking delightful walks through the first snow fall
Smiling at every thought while remembering times past
We delight in the beauty of time
We know the leaves will fall in Fall
The rain will caress us, nurturing our being
The snow will tickle our noses and freeze our toes
The love we received from it all, will soothe our soul

YESTERDAY'S RAIN

The forest trees slumped with yesterday's heavy rain
The waters weep from lashes thick with dew

Tulips lost their petals to the earth given floor
Our lips held softness unexplainable views
Marshmallow soft held the kiss of silk

Water continued to weep over the branches in the forest
The birds chirped bringing in the sunshine of tomorrow
The sky glistened with sparkles usually found on deserts
The night took on a most unusual glow
Puddles dried by the sun made walkways passable
Overhead the galaxy glistened to brighten the way
from the forest which grew thick with over brush
that opened the lashes for a wider view
The love which poured overhead surrounded all living things
Yesterday's Rain brightened all tomorrows
knowing and believing all things are possible
when you let the rain wash away the uncertainties of life
you will live once again for love conquers all

INNER BEING

INNER BEING

Grains of sand caress feet worn toes
Separating them by rolling waves brushing in and out of them
Impressions left behind

Gazing over shores of white capped waves
Splashing on distant rocks
A lone seagull flies

Shadows of clouds overhang a blanket pale blue sky
Awakening of a new day
I sit and wonder
What lay beneath the coral reefs?

A silent heart
Sifting the salty air
Leaving footprints in the sand
Standing – gazing
Feelings of warmth

Listening to the music of the sea
Eyes that don't see – I smile

Always With Me

Like the blossoms that come in spring
Or the river that runs continuously
More so when the rain brushes its' wings
The joy of you and your laughter
Filling the empty cup of day
I think of you

On a clear day you shine through
Like the morning sun warming my heart
You capture and warm my soul

The softness of the breeze that flows past
The joy of knowing you thought of me

The lightness of my every step
Softens the earth's growth

Feelings of your beautiful heart
Overflows mine with silken shadows of love
Wrapped in the hold of another's wish

BEHOLDING

So as it came to pass
From the breath of the Ocean
To the bosom of the Universe
Standing on the shores of the distant Sea
For the tears of the fallen Trees
The Desert in the mist of emotions
As the sand whips vigorously across the vast empty space
Life as it is
Her eyes dance gloriously
And the mind is full with ecstasy
She sees

DELICATE SOUL

The delicate shell holds more than it wants you to know
I see the melancholy bubbles of softness
Flowing through the milky waves of water while the hour glass sifts
The soft breeze that embodies the flowing air
Surrounds and protects the shell
Comfortable within the cycle of life
He moves, with great skill aware of every breath of silence
He marvels at his accomplishments and sweetness permeates from within
The eyes sharp as a Hawk in day and keen as an Owl's ear at night
The heart a cloud of cotton soft tissue filled with love
Holds the cloud close to his breast
The roads he traveled light in touch
Mountains climbed became the path of new adventures
The sea leveling through an ecstasy of rushing waves and depth
Strength and Contentment lay within the Soul covered Shell

Ending of a New

Careful how you handle the next wave
Choose your words with great thought
Understand what you have grown to know
Be silent, listen to the heart
Understanding all that life has given you

Over the past year birth of a new day opened
With the lustrous glow of a rainbow born
Take pride in what was given to you
Understand the depths of its' origin
Know why it had to be this way

Rely on only yourself for guidance
With meditation you will come to know
Remember when the Angels appeared
given the day new meaning
Never lose sight of what they represent

Patience and trust are two glorified lessons
Learned over the traveled years
Flow with the tide or go against it
You have a choice, choose it well

The decision lies with you
The key is to never shut the doors completely
An open heart understands and a captured ear
will bring you to that happy medium

FLOWERING HEART

Although you have left the message
How strong are you connected to staying with it?
Your heart is still opened to receive in a turn of a key
That's the beauty of true love which can't be measured or tamed

Somehow you still find yourself gazing into the open space
The memories bring you peaceful moments of joyous love
Your fingers reach out to yet hold their place

Move, move through the open space
Smile at the purest delights hidden from view but not from you
Listen to your heart
Quiet the soul

Time is a place you make your own
Understand why you have been given this time

The seed was planted in the richest of tissues
No need to water for the body will take care of the flowering blossoms

Put yourself at peace, ease the heart and mind
Nurture the seed
It will Bloom again for the bud is still ripe
Bloom more vibrantly than before

Trust in the Universe for it holds the key to your heart
When it is time, it will be unlocked
For now smile and know you have been blessed
Many journeys over

FOLLOW – FOLLOW

Listen as the notes jump out of the xylophone
and float through the air
Your heart dances with every note
The mind holds the thought
Your body moves to the music from the heart
The heart safely cradles your thoughts
It breathes through and through
Go with it – let it all flow
You are being carried over mountains high
The heart allows the mind to drift
Reminding you that all is possible
and it hears what the mind sees
Listen to the heart
It is the stronger and wiser of the two

HUSH

Thoughts flow endlessly in the early morning hours
The stillness of the overlay of night still abreast
Silence brings so many things into focus
Bound to be still
The mind wonders...this sounds good...
Should I change that phrase?
Dancing with the images
Effortlessly feelings and thoughts come together
As two beings become one...united
Knowing that soon the morning stillness will become frantic with movement
Hold onto the thought; write it down; hold on to the moment
Embrace
Escaping into the unknown you find yourself once again
Whole

IN TOUCH

Pale skies, wet sands – together they move
What is this monumental display of colors?
Vastly moving streams of blue, white, gray, purple and pinks

That settles the restless tides
Soothes the endless soul

Moving from the center of our being
We delight in song
The music we sing dances with our thoughts
Twirling, swirling, twirling

MUSICAL THOUGHTS

When I listen to the soft gentle fingers
gliding across the piano keys
It reminds me of the gentle forest rain falling on the evergreens
With every drop there you are
Smiling at me, letting me know
Here with me always

When I listen to the violin
I hear the soft cotton balls of snowflakes
In the first of winter storms falling briskly on the tree limbs
There again you are smiling at me
I am here smiling back at you my darling

The orchestra plays a melody of symphonies
the whole world is new
The bells are dancing in a circle of love
for me and you

I can see far beyond the horizon
It echoes to me how beautiful you are

When I hear the gentle soft keys of the piano
With fingers softer than silk gliding over them
I know you are always going to be near
My heart sings of joyous days
Alive with spring – alive with you

Rainbow Dreams

Where do you find the Rainbow?
Does it only show itself after a summer thunderstorm?
Through the clouds you will see soft colorful colors

What is under the Rainbow?
You can see more than the eye allows you to
Lie back and gently close the crystal stones that hold your gaze
Let the stillness bring you to your ever loving place

Does it come when you are waking up from an early morning dream?
Can it bring brightness to the saddest of days?
Let the water fall between your spirit
Let your spirit awaken to the dream
Let the dream carry you away

Where do you find the Rainbow?
You can't find it behind the stars
The stars give light, through the night
The Rainbow is wherever you want it to be
Breathe in the air and let the Rainbow come through
The water from the clouds that drip through and through
Will send you the Rainbow brightly new

Under the Rainbow are you
You have all that is needed today
Tomorrow will be what the Angels bring your way
Allow yourself this moment to relax within the dream

Dreaming is your way to escape
to a place where only you know
Open your heart to it all
Comfort the soul
Remember the Angels and know
The Rainbow showers over you always

SILHOUETTE

She moves to the rhythm of the Swan with the wide spread of its' wings
Each step is slow and precise as the hips follow seductively
Her presence creates an element of calmness all around her being
Many eyes watch as she weaves in and out of the crowded room
Words unspoken, yet the eyes follow her every movement
She has grace and elegance
Strength that unfolds within
An air of sophistication and charm caressing her expression
A warm smile from within for the experience is known to her
She lives for the silence as she slowly flows through the room
Gliding through mid-air on wings unseen
Her heart gives way to the softness from deep within
The soft tissues of the full breasted skin
The rapture of it all falls around her sleek sultry body
Like the drizzling rain resting on flames of bright
Her glow creates a rapture of its' own
The love from within permeates the room
She is wisdom and tenderness
Calmness and joy
Understanding beyond the realms of life
She is the delicate soul of a woman in love

So Sad

Can't seem to move from this lonely place
For now its' okay to lay in the quiet of your soul
Never did you think you would feel this way again
Loosing yourself to the moment
Somehow it all seems right
Go, go deep within and sink into the abyss
Let it flow through your veins
Know what no longer is needed, let go, let go
Fall, someone will be there to pick you up
The body is limp, the heart is weak
The mind just moves methodically knowing not where to land
You are graced with someone else's hand
Let the shyness leave its' nest
Take the hand, gently hold onto it
Finger tips to finger tips
Surface, to a joyous day

THE CONVERSATION

Thundering, lighting, wind storms rattling within
Snow flakes, running brooks, morning dew smothering the thoughts
Channeling the rush of it all within the mind
Breathe, breathe..... Let Go
Breathe, breathe..... Let Go
Slowly, gently...... come into focus
Breathe......Let Go
Let the soothing waters engulf your thoughts
Focus......bring to fruition.......
All that is sacred....all you have processed
Let Go...........Let Go
The mind will channel it all with grace and elegance
Be Well........my friend, be well
Smile within for you can open the gates of gold

THE DAY

Throughout the days
We all have many roads to walk
Some days are easier than others

Sometimes unknown until it moves
We can either move with it or let it take over

Some have the ability to flow with the wind
Others know only to stress themselves out
Causing unbearable pain unnecessarily

Believing that all things are possible if we give it a try
Walking on the bright side of everything
Opens our energy to a new light
Vision what it is like

Smile at the day and the day will smile back
Remove your dreams from the pillow
Hold your dreams in your heart

Listen to how they soothe the ache
Take away the sorrow
Bring the flow of energy rushing through
You can carry any day the way you want to
Why carry it without love of yourself

What we find comfort in clearly tells who we are
You are the crystal light that shines
The colors of the rainbow will always glow around you

Carry only what you need
Let the day be

THE VOICE WITHIN

Soothing water falls, brushing over precious stones
Guiding you to wondrous memories of your own
Watching the wind whipping around flying leaves
Twigs and branches falling at our knees
Stones glistening brightly embraced by vibrant colors from the sun
Mesmerized while our sight held still the thoughts
Warming our souls when we were little one's
Memories of old we came to know
Brings back the beauty of falling snow
We hear what our mind sees
See what our ears hear
We are destined to be who we are
For out of the womb life becomes our own
All that we see, all that we hear, all we have done
Brings us to what we hold dear
Smile Within

THOUGHTS OF YOU

I watch as my hand glided across the paper
Writing to the sounds of a distant violin playing
It soothes my soul and my fingers hold the pen ever so gently
As if I was caressing your face
You smile and my heart smiles back
Your soul has traveled today and I saw it leaving
My heart stopped for seconds on seconds
Will you return to the comfort of my arms?
They are waiting to hold your delicate soul
The candle burns inside and the flame is warm
The heart never dies
The violin brought in the symphony of souls
Together they glided with my pen
The music was a scene to never let go
You are here – I feel your being
Precious life so precious is life

You Are

You are the Temple of your being

The crystal light within
The meadows of bloom
The sea henceforth you came from

You can change all, by a single thought
For your beauty is the life force
Your courage is to know
Your Will is what you do with it all

All you have done, you have done well

The Goddess of the Temple is who "You are"

YOU

Crystal covered snow
Soul
Musical notes from a symphony
glistening on a violin
Mystical
Joyous moments of joy
Heavenly
Laughter seeping through your words
Smiling
A lightness in your step
A heart filled with warmth
The journey has begun

LETTING GO

BEGINNING TO END

When you miss the beginning
You will never have to worry about missing the end
Everything that happens in the middle will predict the end
The story unfolds and you begin moving through the space
The mind recalls how it all began
The heart beats with the opening of valleys
Rushing fluid to the veins
Bursting with excitement
Your story is told to another
The listener becomes overwhelmed
For life as it is has never happened like this for them
Afraid of revealing their feelings
They distance themselves
The separation is that of an elastic band
You recall the beginning
Knowing you missed nothing in the beginning
The middle became the tug of war
The ending is a familiar stop
No words are forming from the lips
Silence becomes the end

BLESSED BE

Walk in the silence of the day
See in the night
Know what lies ahead

Hold on to what you can - dream
Let go of that which you no longer need
Love and be loved

Cry with the tears that flood the heart
Let them fall over the ripples of sorrow
Cleansing your being
Know you are loved

Run with the wind whipping at your heels
Moving majestically while you are in flight

Turn yourself around and around again
Smile at the day
Love your way

Smile with the Angels
Breathe deep – go deeper
Kiss the day good-bye
Know tomorrow is a new way
Love over and over again
Smile with pure delight

FINDING PEACE

You may never understand how it happens
Understanding life is a start
You walk on heaven's shores
They unfold into the grassy meadows

Take time to listen to the heart
It's a marvelous instrument that plays melodies - listen

Speak not to no one – enjoy the silence
Go within and listen

Time will let you know when to share your heart
Bring in the joy of love to guide you on your way
Don't let the doors close you in
The sun will shine through the windowpane
Warming that which has been uncovered by the cold

Sing, sing gloriously and float through the air
The time is yours and you will find peace
and beauty in all you have touched

Let the teardrop that housed the eyes and covered
the months of waiting fall effortlessly away

Follow the Heart and the Mind will move close behind

Knowing What's Best

You have walked the endless road
Your mind has traveled the tides effortlessly
Know when it is time to cross the stream
You stand there you hesitate the other side holds no promises

Knowing what is best you use the washed up pebbles to steady yourself
Each step a thought for the next

Your heart is heavily weighted – you breathe
The air is still the heart lies with it

Thoughts carry you to days of joyous times
Remembering how the torch was lit – you smile
It is no one's fault the world was turned upside down

Love happened
How wonderful is that, but with it came heartache
We did not wish for our lives to take the unlikable road
We both tried to follow our hearts

Connected over time and hold a presence is a rarity not found often
enough
To love is to be loved back and let nothing hold you from that destiny
Happiness, a gift bestowed only on a few
Unfortunately everyday life over ruled our hearts
Waters carried them beyond

You held out your hand as far as it could reach
There was no one there to hold, love and care for you
The heart needed to smile, keeping the feelings alive
You walked away

Letting Go

The heart lay heavy with untenable feelings of days ago
The body moved methodically around the evergreens
that glistened under the dismal sun
If tomorrow had been yesterday, the clouds would have
shined brightly through the milky gray sky that covered the heart

Thoughts of how it came to pass, what it could have been crowded the mind
Winter held the earth's stillness the body succumbed to the bleakness of it all

The soul held the magical and mystical feelings protected in the womb
covered by a special moment in time

Teardrops filled the emerald stones that dried the faceless face
Silence brought warmth through this massive storm and the day held still
The body no longer breathed feather light
Once again protected by the Womb, which held it all

Moving painfully slow through the whipping wind that blinded
the tear stained soul
Angelic voices whispered soothingly to gently let go

NEVER TO SAY

We are taught many things from birth to adulthood
Some things come very naturally
Some are a challenge throughout our lives

Having a beautiful feeling inside brings out a smile
warm and tender to the soul

A story told of something so unusually funny brings
out the laughter that unfolds

Were we ever told how to grieve?
To know its' okay to cry
That warm tender hug that melted the tears aside

The hardest of all is saying Good-Bye
Why?
Good-Bye is final
Fold the words in a handkerchief and hold it close to your heart
Smell the scents that once held the handkerchief
Never say Good-Bye

When times are blue
Remember to walk in the Rain
The silence of your soul will bring the memories of old to life again
Let the raindrops caress your face and warm your heart
Let the love once felt live within again

ONLY ME

Looking back at what might have been
I see so clearly and ask
Was it only me?

That cannot be
For when I see your face looking at me
It says it was you and me

In the beginning we both felt
it would always be

Our hearts opened to a beautiful world
It was you and me
We created our own world
Where laughter reigned always
Soothing evenings by the fire we lived
Letting our emotions take our hands
to a place where others never dare to chance

We followed our hearts
Realized there could not be forever you and me

A friendship was built
on the wings of you and me

Not sure what that means to you
Know what it means to me

Now there's you
Then there is me

STRANGE AS IT IS

The page lay blank
Thoughts fall under the same link

You try to listen to your heart
The key doesn't turn

Yesterday came and went
Nothing changed

Tomorrow is now here
Nothing has changed

You look at the page and no words fell on it
So much to say – speechless

The pen found a place to silence the noise

THE MISSION

Floating gracefully with the tides
Moving majestically like the hawk
Soaring through the heavens
Going nowhere – yet somewhere
The mission unfolds into a breath taken moment
The wings of heaven lift you to another element
Moving, ever so lightly – you are gliding
Together the rhapsody of knowing
All that surrounds you is exhilarating
You can go anyplace you wish
Imagine the vast empire you are surrounded by
Floating on air – you are life
See what life has in store for you
Don't hold back move with it all
Higher grounds and wisdom you have gained
Be patient – let the waters flow swiftly, gently over you
It all comes together in one flick of a move
The heavenly Angel has guided you this far
Continue to trust – life has no limit
You are love – you have loved – you will love again

Wait No More

How long do I wait?
I have waited an hour and a day
Or more my way as the days move on
Through months and months
Almost a year to the day
I have waited

For it not that I know your heart
I would not be waiting
How long does this waiting period last?

Until the tides no longer rush to shore
Or the rain no longer falls
There is no answer because the heart
feels it all and moves you to where you need to be

You toss and turn in the middle of the night
Fighting the yearning of being close to
the one you are in love with
Then the rain falls
Bringing the rushing tides to shore

You continue to wait because you know the heart
of another and he knows yours

When the rain no longer falls
Or the tides no longer bring the waves to shore....
 You wait no more

WHAT HAPPENED

Where has the time gone?
I no longer see the sun shining
Eyes wide open blinded by the mist
Once over twice you held me within your gaze

I no longer see you looking at me
You have moved to a place beyond reach
Did life pass us by?
Or was it the foolishness of our hearts
closed by sight with our tomorrows swept away

The days are quiet without your laughter
Your great sense of humor always brightened anyone's day

When I gaze upon your garden, the flowers tell your story
The birds that nestled within them
no longer fly in the fields

Fonder memories I could have never had
Without you in my life

WHERE AM I GOING

Lying in the hollow of your heart
You hear the distant sounds of the storm
passing through
The sky turning colors of blues to grays
Gray the soothing color of white softness

Birds take flight as the storm passes through
Flocking to wherever their wings will carry them safely out of view

You dream you can do the same
You lay in sweet slumber waiting for your wings
to take you above the earthly plane
Slowly your body is in flight and you can travel
beyond the realms of life
Knowing you are safe in your world
You rest your dreams upon a pillow star

The eyes now closed to hear clearly the sounds of smiles
You rejoice as you know this is your world
The Universe is moving you from one end to another
in this vast open space of calm
The tears you wanted to shed drip from view
You cradle yourself in the comforts of your thoughts
Wonder where you go from here

WITHIN

The rain came in heavy drawls all through the night
The grounds in the morning lay dry with sight
Gusty winds and thunder filled the air
Was it rain or sorrow that I felt so near?
Or the need to hold onto someone so dear
Lightening flashed over again and again
Did I see that or imagined what I felt within
The grounds lay dry in the mist of the storm
Teardrops fell, the body was still
I walked in sadness because of my will
The grounds lay dry and that was true
As my body and mind carried the storm through
In the wake of morning, I mourned no more
Past days, months, and years of sorrow gone
Life holds within what you have known
My soul a vessel as I am reborn

Your Eyes – Your Smile

I never knew what love could be until I looked deep
into those crystal blue eyes
Then you smiled at me
I never hungered before until you were gone
Life without you is the flower that never bloomed
The waterfall that never flowed
Your words pierced my ears like the roaring thunder
"I don't want to begin something I can't finish"
The beginning had already taken place
Confused and torn on accepting fate as it is
I'm alone no one returns my calls
When last we met
I came because I knew my heart could carry yours
To a place where all is calm and beautiful
I would have never let you go for when I fell
in love with you it was for eternity
Never did I want to turn the river upside down
Knowing you're gone
Words
I have none to share

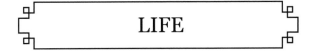

LIFE

ANOTHER DAY IN TIME

What happened to the morning joy?
Life was so simple and then your world was crushed
How did I let this happen?
I opened up my heart to a wonderful man
Waited endlessly for hours, days, weeks and months that passed
Never giving up hope that he would come rescue me
Knowing what others see in me
I didn't want to be out there by myself again
Did he understand the pain and anguish that had settled into my heart?
Did I have a complete understanding of his needs?
I had more than empathy in his walk on earth
Understanding him beyond the barriers of living
Understanding his needs– could I fulfill them? – of course
Would he let me – pulling away – powerful source of strength
Afraid of what – nothing will harm you as long as I am here
and you are there for me
I think of the others who walk this earth as "wolves"
Traveling in packs with their tongues dragging the ground
Waiting, anxiously waiting for the opportunity to pounce on me
I want which I cannot have
I asked for nothing and nothing is what I received
Was the strain of being connected too much to apprehend?
What was he searching for in the early hours of meeting me?
Life is complicated enough – then you fall in love

A New Day

I watch as the water slowly drips between
my fingertips
Leaving soft splashes upon the pavement below
Like that of the tears that leave my eyes
They no longer see you
Feel you, how I long to feel your touch
Going to that special place in my mind
All will be as it was meant to be
I feel your energy surrounding me
The touch is familiar and warm
We haven't left one another
We are traveling to the rush of our
feelings from years that once was lost
We are dancing in the wind to a new awareness
The swirls of our grace wrapping around
our souls
Yesterday's love came again and moves with
tomorrows wishes that were blown to the wind
caught in a blissful surge of energy
Your grace has lavished my being with
ecstasy once again
No longer do I have to dream
The tears have turned into loving memories
of melted ice
The purity and rarity of our love sustains all

GRACEFUL STEPS

I no longer feel the hunger
that once was felt when I was
not by your side

When I walk the shorelines
I find comfort listening to the
waves that swish back and forth

When the radio plays a beautiful love song
I take pleasure in knowing I loved
from the heart and I will love again

Life smiles upon me and opens the way
to flow with the tides of grace
off again on another glorious journey

My heart dances to the sounds of joy
coming from my heart
and I know what I experienced
was needed to test the waters

Now I can float above all the rough edges
of the given world and rest on a bed of roses

I have lost nothing for there is only pleasure
in knowing love will find me again

Holy Land

What does it mean this special place!!!
Covered by millions of footprints
Centuries ago it belonged to all
Now held prison by one

Conquered by many and ruled the same
Blood stained sands that blow
Surround streets of yesterday
Once were dressed in gold

When peasants walked like Nobles
Nobles cast their spell
The Heavens' heard the rumble like thunder in the clouds
The Holy man above all men walked beside them all
Teaching love and kindness to all his flocks of old and young

The Holy land flourished with the richness of His wisdom
We became His disciples to carry out His will
Your will be done He said unto you
For He is always there to carry us through
The Holy Land once was will be
The resting place of all mankind

KNOWING THYSELF

When you feel the harsh thunderous words stab your heart
Like the crackling sounds of lightning
Or the emptiness you feel from unkind words
Taking the life from beneath your feet
You will always find comfort in knowing who you are
For the universe holds many elements of strength
For those who wish to crush your spirits
Knowing yourself - nothing holds dearer
Knowing who you are
What you do for others
Isn't measured by your deeds
The tenderness of your heart
Will always be there to comfort you
The depth of your soul will glow
Amidst the grey clouds that once shattered your hopes
Breathe a silence of joy
Gifted from one most high

LADY IN BLACK

There in the corner sat a Lady in black
The tapestry that hung on the windows was French in fact
She sat very quietly watching them come and go
Wondering what stories they would tell
Fancy the colors of all the delicious conversations
She sipped her cocktail while her gaze swept the room
Her eyes moved mysteriously, her ears heard it all
Those in the background, oblivious to her call
She imagined the room with her eyes closed
Faces and personalities surrounded her in the dimmed lit room
Wisdom and elegance she was, unnoticed as she enjoyed it all
A delicious dish served when the conversations fell to whispers
Like a chameleon she blended with the colors in the room
Ate of the delectable conversations

LIFE GOES ON

When I walk by your garden
The warmth and joy I no longer feel
The joy from your presence has vanished
I walk in silence and see the world
The sound of music is no longer heard
Where the flowers grew is only empty
rows of spacious ground where once they lived
I view you in a different light now
You have traveled outside the protected walls
that held you close to my being
You are not forgotten
Our journey is over

LIFE HAPPENS

We don't always wish for what comes to us
It happens
We have so many mountains to climb
and rivers to cross
Then the rugged terrain that we gallop through
Sandy beaches we sink our body into
Many walks under the raindrops
The fallen snow that embraces our inner souls
We ask for none of this - life happens

Storms will always pass by
We awaken to a new dawn
Making sure we have missed nothing
When our life has been taken from us
We stand in that higher place
Gaze upon what could have been
Hoping we fulfilled all our dreams
Today we live for ourselves
Before the days leave us

MOMENTS

They come and go like the snow flake that doesn't know where to land
A gust of wind carrying your thoughts to the universe
The moment passes
What you thought about has significant meaning
Soon to leave the nest
The moment comes back like the warm breeze
that just wisped by your face
You wait for it all to pass
The waiting can become painfully exhausting
Wonderfully exciting
Let it pass, let it pass
No matter the wait, it is always worth it
What you make of the moment is yours
Thoughts will always be in the moment
The waiting will test the moment
You my friend will flow through it all

NIGHT RIDERS

They move with the speed of light
Mission - they are on a mission
The quest is to conquer
Waters carried them to distant shores
Weapons held high
They are mighty – they are one
Shields protect them – guarded by the Angels
They thrust forward – knowing that some may not be saved this day
Shores will carry the fallen to a higher plane
Ancestors look over them for all is in the hands of the Gods
The hooves that carry them seem to glide over the earthy terrain
Swords drawn – they move on
Taking down what no longer has a purpose
They are one – they are one
The strength of all combined a nucleus of love and determination
The earth has awakened – the heavens are alive
The wings of the Angels have helped them on this quest
Freedom

Remembering

You woke to the beautiful music of a cardinal perched outside your window
The sweet smell of spring teasing your nostrils
Games of pleasure which delighted your heart
Hopscotch, jumping rope, marbles and tiddlywinks
All was magical, all was delightful
Pick-up sticks, wonder ball and jacks
Home cooked meals that warmed our hearts and filled our souls
Hand-me-downs, you were proud to wrap your body in
The Shadow Knows played once a week on the radio
Coming home from school to see the one person you held so dear
waiting for you in the cool warm air
Life was simple and fun
What happened over the years where life was like fresh brewed beer?
Sundays were truly a day of worship
Department and grocery stores were closed
What you needed on Sunday, you purchased on Saturday
You were home, no television or computers and maybe some had radios
A good book to read
Paper dolls to play with or those lovely coloring books
Close your eyes and just think back
Remembering When...

Someone Special

You know when that special someone
walks into your life
You awake in the early morning hours
With the rain pouring from the heavenly sky
You only see the sun shining
Life became real – real became you
Like the opening of a flower – you have blossomed
All that surrounds you sings with joy
Your heart is like a violin playing on the strings
You smile for you are loved
The beauty you find in others shows through your soul
Captured by Cupid all is elegantly wondrous
The flow of the cords within the heart
bring beautiful sounds – and you dance
Your heart touches the music – twirling, twirling
Gifted beyond the realms of earth
You fly gracefully above the clouds
Resting peacefully on the puffed cushion
Waters of rushing winds of wings you sing again
Nothing can break the thread between the folds of life
For the journey has been slow but so promising

THE ARTIST

Her words moved swiftly over the blowing winds and she
watched as the cotton swayed back and forth
Waiting patiently for the thoughts to form drifts in the mind
Like sand dooms on a desert floor
Pressed fingers caressed the helpless pen
trying to capture the minds thoughts of years past
The mind guiding the pen across the unbleached parchment,
expressing feelings of emotions that lay beneath the troubled heart
Lightly, gently the heart pumps and the blood flows easily through
Like the fluttering wings of a hummingbird
Moments so special hung in mid-air resting aimlessly
Sad memories seeped through the unleveled waves of silent
The mind held it all
The past unchanged - tomorrow a struggle,
Today held the helpless pen and the future will come with peace one day
With spring comes those enchanted vibrant colors on flower beds that
slept through the winter storms
With unspoken words, blank parchment, the artist basked in the delight of
bittersweet love of friendship between two

THE MIND

I gazed upon the unshapely clouds that moved systematically by
The day held bewitching feelings of the dismal tides
My eyes found a place to rest my "Whys"

THE MOMENT

The moment came without a thought
Thought became the glow
The glow that nourished our beating hearts
Became the beam which, housed our dreams
A Déjà Vu, a quick look back
From whence it came to pass
The thought a memory held our hearts
and soothed our beautiful souls
Brought enchanted music to our lips
So much we do not understand
We walked the endless path
The Moment came to be
We saw between the glowing thought
The Moment
Lost in the winds of light

THE TEARDROP

A drop of wetness forming a beautiful pear shape bubble
With a thin layer of skin surrounding the outer walls
Eyelids filled with an overflow of moisture
Seen when emotions swell up within the mind or heart
Sometimes not knowing how to escape those massive feelings
They come in drawls like the whipping wind carrying years of hurt
Or the hurricane that just rushed the ocean over the sea line
Ripping branches off trees and crushing them to the ground
It could be the warmth from the daily sun
Or the serenity of the moonlit sky carrying the galaxy to a distant land
Taking our emotions with it and dropping them into the desert sand
Laughter brings a joyful tear to our eyes
Unable to hold the joy of it all when it escapes from deep inside
Overwhelmed with such wondrous joy we burst into tears
from the sight of it all
A clear crystal watery bubble pouring out from the lids of lashes
Cleansing our bodies like the soft flowing snow flakes cleanses the earth
A precious jewel that we have the willingness to create by will or uncontrollable emotions

THE VISION

See it for what it is and not what you want it to be
Focus on the Vision
Bring it into your mind
See it for what it is
Live for the moment
Leaving the "what ifs?" behind
Bask in the beauty of what enters into your life
Question not and follow your heart
Move with every beat of it
The mind will find a way to honor the heart

THE WILL

We grasp for what we cannot have
Have for not we want
What brings us to this unpredictable place?
The mind carries a will of its' own
Whereas the heart rules the throne
Tomorrow is an endless time for not today
As we ponder and play
Honor the Goddess of your Temple
The Temple will carry everything its' way

THEIR WORLD

They sat in a world of their own
Above the clinking sounds of their spoons hitting
the sides of their bowls of cereal

Rhythm of sounds
Precision without machinery

Words were spoken
Yet nothing was heard

Satisfaction received with every mouthful consumed

The silence of their souls sitting tougher made their morning
A magical delight

THROUGH PAIN AND SUFFERING

The storm lay heavy over the clouds, no sounds to be heard
Silence groomed the heavens
The clouds of moving grace gave way to a bleak and dismal day
then night fell
In the distance cries of pain rang through the silence
The world was in turmoil and the escape was none
The cries rang out again
Surrounded by the evildoers those of many walked in sadness
Afraid to intervene forsaken their life to end
Fallen on knees bent as their bodies could no longer hold them up
Through the pain and suffering
The clouds broke their silence as the words rang from them
The rain came in thunderous drawls of rhythm for days, weeks
He was saved and gave us eternal life
It was written – life will reign in a higher place
The earth and all its' habitants will know
What they have done this day
Gave testament for tomorrow lay

UNTOUCHED

Glistening sounds over wind swept sands
Under the ripples of waves casting shadows overhead
Refreshing feelings untouched from years past
Warms the tucked away flesh of yesterday
Unfolding into an ecstasy of a waterfall
Caressing stones as the water flows over them
Moving gently through the heart of the soul
Sensuously bringing joy to every touch
Your body melts like butter in summer
Fields of fragrant joyous flowers fill the air
Embracing the fulfillment of life together
When the souls become entwined as one
Breathlessly, the bodies unfold
Wrapped in a cocoon of silk lace
You found your place

WAITING

Gazing beyond the realms of life
The wind still blows softly
The air a delicate scent of roses opens the heart
Through the clouds your face appears
Teardrops fill the lids of lashes
Crystal blue the pain gently flows through
Feather light your body gracefully moves
There is beauty in your graceful flight
Together we grace the earth
Let the sounds of joy hold you
The lashes will flush the teardrops from their cup
Feel the warmth of love surrounding you
Know who waits for you...

WHEN THEY MEET AGAIN

We grasp for those feelings of life again
Our hearts are warmed by those soft fleeting moments
When one touch from your loved one caresses the soft delicate skin of yours
Remembering the gentle hand that smoothed the facial skin
Wrapped its' arms around you so lovingly
Tranquility flowed through our veins like that of a running brook
pouring its' waters over bright green brush and gentle stones with blossoms
blooming in early spring, bringing warm colors of light to the eye
We hold those precious moments so close to the heart
For warmth and love are essential when you are in love
The body spoke and the heart listened
We moved to the music of our heart and the moment
brought sensual feelings of love to life again
The mind will always remember those precious moments
The absence of your lover moves those precious moments
within the layers of your soul
The long waited days and nights to reunite the two hearts again
Your mind begins to wonder of the possibilities
The heart knows that love will prevail
For that of the two lovers, true words hold it all together
The heart has no boundaries when love comes to know
With the heart and soul working together
There is only room for love to grow

YOU AND ME

You walked into my life and it changed amazingly bright
When I walked past the garden it was bursting with joy
The tulip opened and blew me a kiss
Remembering that early evening when you blew me a kiss
The daffodil let me pick it and I played
He loves me, he loves me not
The willow tree no longer wept
Spring became Fall
Falling leaves brushed my face
Reminding me when once you caressed my face ever so gently
Fall soon became winter
I smiled as I caught the snowflakes on my tongue
Remembering our first kiss
Winter embraced the warming of the fireplace blaze
The sun showed through
Time stood still for me and you
No longer did the heart hide from view
Your soothing words and gentle touch
opened a beautiful moment of days for me
My heart is still singing
While the raindrops fall from my eyes
Gloriously we will get by
There was so much in the Angels message
and they still fly with us

LOVE

A September Night

As the silhouette moves behind the screen
The light is the movement without a scene
Images of the body as it moves before the light
Who in essence carries himself as being carefree, not quite!!!
He bask to know the performance gives no clue
For the shadow only forms a statue of his moves
He walks alone, with a distinctive stride on the beaten
Paths' of many Passersby
Hands in pockets, clutched out of sight
A smile makes way to reassure his friend is alright
Yet the mind is choking from the thoughts hanging high
His display of aloofness doesn't hide the fight
The words rang out as music held them tight
The silhouette in the light held it all out of sight
The uncertainty and the sureness struggling to keep it right
He reaches out to touch the emptiness of the night
As the heart fluttered and skipped with every fleeting step
He walked the wayside in the breezy fall night
Hearing the crackling sounds of the fire burning upon the man-made looms
That seemed to carry an uncertainty, yet everlasting enchanting tune
And the Lady smiles while devouring the sweetness of this graceful eve
She knows she can rest a year of thousands for all that was seen
Giving thanks to the Angels who are always at her side
She slowly moves around the being and smiles a thousand's delights

A SPECIAL MOMENT IN TIME

I opened my eyes to a beautiful moment in time
While my heart opened with them
Eyes as green as crystal emeralds glowed in the light
Mixed with the second pair of eyes carrying the color of blue topaz
Gave our hearts a new flight

Unexpectedly there you were so strong and tall
Watching over me and making sure I was safe
When you held out your hand, no words were spoken
I took hold and smiled
Yes, I will travel the rivers with you

You captivate my soul
I am yours forever and a day
Wrapped in the loving cove of your body
I lay while you caressed me and kept me from harm
Your ever loving touch holds me so gently
And when you leave, you take not the warmth you gave
Or the laughter we enjoyed with each other

We have something so special
So wonderfully special

We give peace a new meaning
For you can't have peace without true love

Like the river, our love is endless
The journeys we have traveled together are timeless
Knowing the stars will always shine when we are near
Knowing love will always be there

A VERY SPECIAL MOMENT

It was a fleeting moment
when the two became one
Their hearts moved through the haze
that hung over the area where they rested upon

Through the tall evergreens that lay to one side
engulfed an area for wild life to graze
Filled the air with a freshness of movements within the
softly moving breeze of the day

As the sun found its' way to shine through the day
lying heavy with an uncertainty of future days

He strolled in and out of the charismatic area
casting warmth, only a lover would understand and feel
I viewed him so tenderly and he caught my heart once again
As he viewed one ever so true

The words under the flushed lips found a way to
rest behind the tongue and the mind knew not to
bring forth that which pondered the heart

Gentle moments were unwrapped under
the love of two crystallized gems
Bringing the day to light

ALWAYS HERE FOR ONE ANOTHER

You are the heavens in the sky
That melts my heart like a blossom washed by the rain
You take my life and hold it gently in your hands
You watch over me whenever I am around
So delicately sweet of love for another

I see the gentle soul that you are
I see the heart that needs the comfort of another

Let me comfort you whenever you are in need
I will bring you the ecstasy you for many years have longed for
My heart will wrap its' precious warmth around yours
Soothing out the worries of the days gone by
and brightening the days to follow our footsteps

Precious are the tides that brought us together
With such unbelievable understanding of each other
We are truly blessed by our fortune of golden years
There is a heaven because we are here experiencing
the wonders of the given life

Let me brush the string of worries from your being
Let the day bring no despair
Awaken to that which you know is here
Open your heart and let the emotions flow
to another who needs her heart caressed as well

All that we have, all that we know, all that we need
is right under the hearts that bring us peace
Let me hold you and I will let you caress me
Like no other has ever been able to do
The way we are is the way we were meant to be

AROUND

Thoughts of you crowd my heart
The mind follows the stream of the flowing waters
Casting a glowing light upon the wind
Knowing you're always there for me
Even when I throw you away
Smiling at my foolishness
Two delightful hearts
Given way to the sun
Holding our time together
As one

BEAUTY SURROUNDS YOU AND ME

Today I love you the same as yesterday
Tomorrow will be what we make of it
The future lies under the wind
And you have brought me to this day

Knowing that what we have is beyond our pillows of dreams

When I no longer see
I will always feel
Feelings are so heavenly light

Our hearts glow like the stars in the night
resting their hearts on the brightest one

We swim through the winds of tides
As we drift by and by
Watching the sun rise
We have given of ourselves to nature
Nature has given us the universe
We surpass what others struggle for
Feather light, carefree and bright

We are the moon on any given night

BELIEVE AND TRUST

Wish, Wish and Wish again
Once was is no longer – for the moment
How sad the soul
It weeps in stillness
It carries a yearning of "why?"
The comfort no longer lives within
The joy has found a place to cover itself
Laughter is under the skin
How much can the body hold?
All I suppose....
No long – No longer
See the beauty in all things
Look deeper and you will find
Remember the joy that filled the heart
How the two laughed together
Loved together
Believe that all things are possible
This heaviness will soon pass
You will come to know
What was planned for the two, was planned a long time ago
Believe – Trust – Believe

Embracing Love

To hold it in mid air
To share the feelings with them
To walk in the rain forest and breathe
Ecstasy in the flow of emotions
Wrapping around your hearts
The gentle hand caressing your face
The bond between the two lovers
Gloriously we travel the roads unknown to future lay
Looking into velvet eyes of glistening precious stones
Smiling back at you
Knowing you are truly loved
Beauty is found in the folds of our rippling feelings
We move together as one

ENDLESS LOVE

Listening to the rain fall against the windowpane
Watching how it slowly cascades down
Creating a look like that of a mirage
Moves so seductively
Making bellowing circles around the open space

Candlelight from the room cast a
sensuous glow through and around the window

The serenity of the given space fills your being
The smile that permeates out of you is lustrous love
You reminisce of days past and your heart is aglow

Feelings of warmth, tender loving warmth wrap their arms around you
You are pulled into the open arms of another
You smile over and over again

Stay where you are in the special moment of time
Be with it and open your heart
And the heart will open to you and more

Endless Love is what you feel

Flow of Emotions

It happened – wasn't planned – just happened
A surge of warm lustrous feelings rushing through your veins
Draining every drop of blood
The warmth covered the cold lonely days that followed
Your whole being rejoiced with knowing
The wings of your ecstasy carried you on high
Bubbly so bubbly
Smiles enlightened your presence
The brightness of your being is noticed by all
You are swimming in Love
What wondrous joy unfolds around you
Your whole body wrapped in a tissue of softness
Floating through the air and the wings are carrying you
Anticipation awaits the knock on the door or the telephone to ring
Your heart flutters, your knees buckle, the warmth of a beaming smile
appears
Remain calm control yourself from jumping into his arms
You are in "Love" glorious precious "Love" beholds the two of you

FOLLOW YOUR HEART

Moving from one emotion to another
How do you hold it all together?
Thinking you have it all in the palm of your hands
Somehow the palms hold only air

Move again in the twirling wind of air
Thoughts carry you to a safe haven
You know what's best
You do just the opposite

What is comfortable to you may not be for others
You follow your heart and the mind is confused
Then you follow the mind and the hearts rhythm is confused

Emotions race through and through the open heart
The open heart is pure and true
The mind wrestles with all that comes through

How do you hold it all together?
Choices, so many choices
You can fall deep into the cup or hang outside of it
Does it really matter what you do?
Only you know what's best

Wisdom of the heart and mind is what will show you

Never lose sight of your loving heart
The mind will sort the words that are carried from the heart
Tomorrow is a new Day to Shine

FORBIDDEN FRUIT

That which hangs from the vine
Ripened juices that lay within the succulent morsels
Holds a taste unknown
Expectations of how long until the sweetness escapes
Endlessly longing to enter into that succulent pleasure
The internal feelings held close to the heart
Ripened juices pour over the vine and into a delicacy, divine
Leaving a sweetness delighted to the touch
Raptures of the unknown love settle with the embracing of life
Endless breaths and joys of ecstasy as the bodies taste of the vines' juices
Now ripened from the juices of love
No longer forbidden

HEAVEN

I always knew there was a Heaven
Then I met you
Over years of traveling far
We were back together again
Older, wiser and much more understanding

The gates were not opened to me on that bleak and draining eve
Then the Angels sang like a mocking bird
We are not ready for you my dear
We have closed the gates

Go, go find him
He is waiting for you
You know you have wanted to be with him a year of Sundays
Too many years have passed and now it is time

Let him know you are here
Bring life to two souls who have traveled many journeys high

Be present with Love an understanding
Be ever so patient for he is a delicate soul
and loves you more than you know

My darling, my darling, my darling
I will give you the time needed to unwind the twine
For love is the emerald jewel of you

How Love Feels

The dossal tree lie baron under the fallen leaves of fall
The sky stripped of its' beauty under the gray blankets that
tucked the voluminous white clouds away
To know that blossoms would come in spring and flowers would grow in summer
Your heart sings
The years passed without a thought or feeling of what love could be
The heart opens like a tulip feeling the succulent sweet wet dew upon its petals
As the loved one gently kisses your cheek
Lustful butterflies flutter flirtatiously by as they play
a melody from a piano concerto
And you marvel as you watch a stone skipping across the silky water
Leaving pockets of bubbles in the air
While the horizon captures your whispered thoughts
Knowing the unspoken words move gently across the universe to perched ears
Silence, emotions held still, you pause in thought and as they escape
You hear the sweet music from a wind chimes, sweet, sweet music
You smile, you know how love feels

JOURNEYS

Let the rain fall on any given day
Let the evening sunset in mid-October soothe your mind
With the vibrant colors of autumn
Take a walk along the shore when dawn breaks
Reminisce of your years journeys
Bring back the smiles that have nestled within
The rain will always wash away sadness
The autumn leaves will brush by
When winter arrives and the snow falls
Let it warm your heart
Your life has been many wondrous years of travel
Reflects a journey well spent
Masters have come and gone
and have taught you well
You have brought their teachings to many
The walks have been ever so precious
You have learned to be humble and have endured
no more than others
Although at times it may not seem that way
Knowing the most precious element of life
Is the everlasting love that has been with you
Brought to life by the man you fell in love with
one December night

KEEPING THE LOVE ALIVE

Moving like the waterfall
Over rocks and streams
Chasing dreams
Where are they going?
Can I catch them?

I find myself running and running some more
The wind is blowing in my face
My hair is flowing in the breeze
I am free and my life is mine

I am so alive because I live and live more
and more each day

Happily loving where I am
Rolling in fields of flowers
Sweet smelling flowers
Someone is watching me
Smiling at me
I run to him
His arms wrap around my body
Hold me, hold me, never let go
Love me, never stop loving me
I'll never stop loving you
Free, we are free
Joyously in love
Safe when I am with you
Watching over me always
I smile from the heart

KISS OF THE SUNFLOWER

Let your mind go and travel the world
The wonders you will encounter are breath taken
Your moves are elegant and peaceful
Simply lift yourself up, higher and higher
You are blissfully beautiful in spirit

Open the heart and see all
Know when to sit and be in the love given space
Breathe deeply, smell the air and its raptures
Live in the moment

Gently smile on the "kiss of the sunflower"
Know he was holding your heart so tenderly
in his and that is where it will lay safely

Lift your body to the heavens and fly
Spread your wings and take the love above the clouds
rest in the heart of them
Know you are very special for what has been given to you

The moment will live on forever within your soul
His will always unfold around yours
Inseparable
Love for Life

LISTENING TO THE HEART

We moved together once again in time
Time was ours
We reminisced of past years
Held each other without touching
Our hearts glistened with the joy of another day
The day became days of days to always remember

I had not known I would stop by
There you were, watching over me
So lovingly, so tenderly
You bring me peace you bring me love and so much joy
I could have danced all around the room

Many surrounded us
It was only two in the room that mattered

Watching your lips move and that beautiful smile
as you spoke to me
Brought such a sensational feeling within

At last you pulled me close to your warm
sensual loving body
Lost in the bliss of loving joy I melted in your hold

You bring me life on a gentle wind
You bring me all that I need

Angels guide us, we just have to listen
ever so warmly to their words that are carried across the heavens
True love has no boundaries we are free spirits

LOVE AND LIFE

The dismal days of life ahead
Washed by the clouds of snow
Covered trees at last no growth
Shadows all we know

Winter is upon us
The smell of seasoned wood caressing our senses
Warms our toes with delight
Cuddling close to one another

Within the soul nestled love, feelings grow
We thought we knew what once we felt
Would never come again
Amidst the changes in our lives
Paradise blooms within

Hour to Hour – Day to Day
What we have will always be, for within the walls of love
Nothing is as sacred then thee

Love In Winter

Winter is upon us with twinkling snowflakes that sing
What joy, what fun to run, frolic, in the happiness it brings
Cozy winter nights, by the fireside we love
Romantic nights forever, lovers in love
Memories of old and new ones to come
We welcome all this and more in the December sun
Smiling, crying, and hugging ever so tight
I dream of yesteryear, all that it held
Knowing tomorrow is a mystery of faces untold
A thought of what it was and would be what it's not
Keeps a warm loving smile within my open heart
Yesterday the joy while tomorrow moves it on
A teardrop forms on the emerald green stones dripping onto
lashes as thick as the evergreens that grow
A warm smile sweeps away the pain as joy brushes the stones
For love smooths the wrinkles in the worn out heart of one

LOVE IS NEVER LOST

You found me on a summer morning
I found you the same way
We crossed the river together
Our lives intertwined
We held close to our emotions with each other

Try as we did, we couldn't let go
A greater force was holding us together
It poured over our precious beings

We smiled at the day and loved tomorrows way
We journeyed to another shore
We saw our love grow and grow

The blossoms bloomed all year round for us
The trees reached to the sky
The sun always shined through the pouring rain
The snow never made us cold
We had each other to keep warm

For us the day lived forever in our hearts
I loved you and you loved me
Unspoken words need never to be heard
For our hearts told the story
Love is never lost

LOVE

To hold a ray of light in the palms of your hands
Marvel at the colors of the rainbow in the sky
Catch a butterfly on the tips of your fingers
Secretly smiling until it flies away
Or the early morning dew resting on a tulip
The soft breeze of spring flowing through your wispy hair
A smile from a stranger warm and sincere
Is this what love brings?
With the sadness of loss, there brings the joys of tomorrow
Love, we need not search – for love will always find us
Yes, this is love and much, much more

LOVING YOU – YOU LOVING ME

Capturing the feeling of loving someone
It's not something you can hold in your hands
It's a feeling resting in your heart
From the heart it travels to your mind
From there it cascades throughout your body
Like ripples of water flowing from a waterfall
Tingling feelings run through your being
Your smile becomes full of life
Brightening everyone you touch
The walks you take hold so much meaning
Each step glides over fields of joy
Peace has nestled within
You lay back and move to the rhythm
the heart has created
Beauty found in the rapture of two
Quietly, the gentle touch caresses your body
Through the universal forces your body is held
by another
The warmth of another soothes your being
Always within the folds of a loving embrace
You are with me and I am with you

LOVING YOU AS I DO

Loving you has brightened all my tomorrows
The yesterdays have been just as they were meant to be
The future will bring us to an everlasting joy

How many ways to say "I Love You"
By looking into your tender loving eyes of warmth
Caressing the moment
Holding the glow that flows gently through the wind
Knowing you're with me always

When the silence of the heart speaks
You hear every chime like jewels glistening in the winter sun
As the snow shines brightly with streaming colors of the rainbow
Or is it the tulip that caught the morning dew
and sprinkled your heart with joy so new

Those beautiful hands that held the night to morning
The touch so unbelievable soft upon my breast
Lips that held the laughter spilling over us

When you can ride the wind and sing
There is always a lighter day coming our way
Being lifted by your touch and watching the stars move
through the galaxy of darkness

Just the thought of being near you
Knowing you're never far from view
Knowing how it felt the first time you caressed my body
Knowing how it felt when our dreams came to light

A thousand kisses to you
As I wait for them to come back to me
Just knowing all this, is how I say "I Love You"

ONE LOVE FOR A LIFETIME

To feel the waves move in and around your being
The love you feel is real
It wraps its' wings around you
Warmth, ever loving succulent warmth
Gentle loving hands moving over your delicate skin, you smile deep within
Every breath you take your body moves with the flow of motion he creates
Your lover comes in and the two move to a rhythm created of its' own
Nothing else exist – the two lost in a breath taking mist
The delicate thrust of him separating you from one world to another
Lustrously melting away all the cares of yesterday and tomorrow
The two move with the waters flowing through
Once one, never again to part for the rapture of sense is still
Stay, stay inside and bask in the light of ecstasy
Filling your hearts with a moment in time
Bond together on the edge of high
Live today and let tomorrow carry you away

POWER OF LOVE

The presence of the unknown yet known to you
Like a warm breeze that caresses the trees
Warming the heart of a flower in bloom
Or was it the sun that melted the snow away
Or the heart that lost its' play
A fallen leaf not knowing where to hide
The evergreen reaching the sky
A romantic look of an unfamiliar passerby
The smile from knowing what's inside
Call it what you want
See it as it is
Know that beyond all depths
It's the love from me to you for years past and those to follow

SAYING "I LOVE YOU"

How to say "I Love You"
Listen to the music of the heart
Did you not hear I called to you?
I love you so many ways
When your limbs move across the room coming towards me
The smile that seeps through those warm tender lips
The beautiful hands that once caressed the side of my face
The gentle way you held me in your gaze
The soft golden locks that crown your head
I remember all too well how I massaged them
The glance from afar watching over me
The soft spoken words that landed on your tongue
Soothing my heart in a rapture all its' own
Watching how you smile within not knowing I feel the warmth
Your energy channeling to me through the cosmic light
Feeling your presence ever so near - watching over me - when you are not in sight
You ask "why do I love thee"
Look at me Darling, look deep within me and you will embrace
the warmest, tender, compassionate sincerest love,
love has ever known
How do I say "I Love You?"
Look into my eyes

Your Absence

As I sit and listen to the most beautiful love song
being played on the piano with eloquent orchestra music
in the background – I realize that weeks have passed and my heart
still yearns for your warmth

Love holds dear what is sacred to us and we loved
without the need of touch. We experienced a special
kind of love affair one could ever imagine. We captured
each other's heart and the heart didn't know where to travel
when silence fell over our spirit.

You hadn't planned on being loved so tenderly. You didn't
know I would leave without a word. My heart could no longer
wait or endure the absence of you.

I wonder what you feel now. I am resting quietly. My mornings
no longer hold you near. I fly with the Angels and find peace
within my soul. My feet barely touch the ground because I float
above the earth now.

I thought without you I would no longer listen to the music that
flows through my heart and there would be no life for me.
I was wrong because my ears are open and I see far beyond the
spectrum of the given light.

I know you...that's why I will always love you....

THE PROMISE

There is so much when those words are spoken
You know from the beginning of each day
As you lie in the early morning hours
Rise to a new day of whispers

There is so much when those words are spoken
You find yourself singing from the music that lies in your heart
You're dancing the world is full of brightness
The smile is for him and all that he is
He carries you through all the roads you walk

There is so much when those words are spoken
The smile from him says more than words could ever say
The touch travels deep and sensuous sensational waves flow within
When his lips press gently upon yours
You melt into a beautiful light of a golden enchanted forest
All has blossomed and continues to grow with love

There is so much when those words are spoken
You hold them to your heart
He arouses a sensational feeling within you as he gently caresses your breast
As he travels the lines of your body
The hands move ever so soothingly across the flesh
You are lifted to another plane

He is gifted beyond this world
There is so much when those words are spoken
"I Promise I will always be by your side"
You smile a thousand kisses of butterflies

THE VISIONARY

Just when you thought the sun wouldn't shine anymore
Your world opened to a beautiful day
The sun rays rang through
Like the stampede of wild horses
You watched as their mane and tails blew to the wind
Their gallop was breath taken
Over the terrain they moved with the wind at their backs
You ran with them and your body moved
swiftly and majestically as they did

Life opened that beautiful window of chance once again
Life was smiling at you
Others noticed the heavenly glow you carried on the flesh
The flesh was as vibrant as the magical colors on stained glass
the first day the two of you met

Elegance and strength walked with you this day
You danced from the heart
Music in the distance brought lightness to your being
The violin mixed with the piano keys
Brought joyous chimes to your ears

You never stopped believing
You never will

Time has its' own time
You are the light of it all
He will come again

TOGETHER

Laying in wake while your delicate skin rests upon mine
We are caught in a lustrous movement of song
Your body slowly, soothingly wraps its glow around mine
Love oh such warmth - sensual love
Created from touch and knowing
Our souls move from one life to another
How we see each other is marvelous
We smile knowing we have found true love
I close my eyes and see you there all around me
Caressing my soul, you have captured my heart
We are breathless
We are love – moving with our unique touch
I feel you again, an again, and again
We are one – turning, turning, over and over again
Hold me, hold me and never let go

UNKNOWN

Saw you passing by
Called to you
You hesitated on coming over – slowly, reluctantly you did

My body felt this unusual feeling of dismay
Longed to be with you – you kept your distance

You were tense when you gazed upon me
I wanted to run to you and wrap my arms around you
to calm the waters inside

Knowing I couldn't for the watchful eyes were upon us
My heart cried out – did you hear it?

Have we left one another or are we just giving space?
The unknown is suffocating my being
How do you feel?
Wishing to get in touch – knowing better than to
Often you come to me in spirit and I love again
Gentle so gentle you are to me....
Lost, so lost am I without you....
Resting all my thoughts with the Angels
I sleep...

Upon a Wish

When we were young at heart
How light our hearts were
We were mesmerized with each other

Flowers were blooming and with them
Our hearts were a bloom too

What we felt was our souls uniting
Gone, gone was your presence
My heart traveled with you
I saw you from afar
Heard you calling to me

You returned on the wings of Angels
delicately carrying you closer and closer to me

You asked for my hand in love
We held on to our dreams and they became reality

Many years later we still loved and loved again
From the womb we gave birth through this marvelous love
Birthing of love of life with each other for all eternally

Cherished moments
Many more years have passed and we are still smiling
Love that was given to us has stayed with us

We sing and dance Hallelujah

WHAT IT TAKES

It only takes a moment when the body starts to tingle
One glorious moment and your heart is floating
Filled with the Angelic music of light
Once it was holding
Then you like a flowering plant burst into spring
The doors to life opened
You will never be the same again
Why would you want to?
For love has captured your heart and yours has captured the flower
To love from the heart and give of the heart
Love pours over you like that of a rushing wave
Rolling back and forth into the cave
Your life now bursting with joy
What more could you wish for?
Only to stay in the moment longer than before

Years of Love

One cannot measure the depth of love
Just flow with it and don't question
It will comfort you and bring you joy
Let your body be swallowed by the feelings
Go with the moment and fly to joy
It will take you to places you never knew
Open your heart and let the feelings come through
Your whole body becomes alive
Smile to the rhythm of the soul
The soul has been here before
Each time so wonderfully new
You are swimming in a pool of sensuous fruit
Delicately, luscious sensual fruit
Breathlessly you move with your soulmate
Embrace the moments and smile
Live
Love again

You Mean Everything To Me

You are the flower within the tulip
The bud that hasn't blossomed
The outstretched leaf to wrap around the vine

You are the soft song of spring
The freeze that winter brings

Imagine life without the colors that fall delicately brings

You are the breath that I breathe

Everything is what you are to me

Your Gardens

I walk through your gardens
You are no longer there
I have looked beyond the flowers and the fruit trees
The Christmas trees labor in the heat
The pumpkin seeds have spread their stems
The roads show tracks where you drove
The sky above holds your love of the fields

I walk through your gardens
You are no longer there
I close my eyes and meditate on where you are
I hold my heart in my hand and see
Far beyond the heavenly sky that has planted the seeds
Your presence is shown to me

I rest my body on the labored land
Gloriously through the clouds you give me your hand
I am pulled miles above
To the safety of your love

I no longer have to walk through your gardens
You have watched for me
As I have searched for you
Your grace is my ever loving space
I am with you – you have always held my love

NATURE

A WHISPER AWAY

I'm the flower that hasn't bloomed
The weeping willow tree that doesn't cry
The sun that hides behind the clouds
The ocean that has no depth
The star that is never seen
The raindrop that never falls
The sand that never blows
The icicle that never freezes
The dew that covers the sky
The air that never breathes
The rainbow that never glows
The bleakest day of winter
that warms the heart
All that is seen and unseen, I can change
I am A Whisper Away
floating through the Universe
Changing the "darkness" to "light"

BEAUTY AND ELEGANCE

We watch as she flutters by
Tantalizing us with her flowing body
Her moves, so graceful and elegant
with each passing flight
Wings of silk flutter endlessly
She swoops in and out of her garden
Tasting all she can and savoring one delight for another day
Like the swift movements of a flash of light
Seen only when she wants us to see
The blossoms in her garden are also our delight
Give birth to all who cherish them
As she gives birth to many
Mademoiselle Butterfly

ENCHANTED

The forest meadows rang with winds of soft bellowing howls
Snow fell lightly on the bare branches
With eyes wide shut you could hear the angels singing a rhapsody of songs
The air moved slowly by

The brush was thick as the snow rested on the earthy floor
A rainbow view seeped through the overhead of trees
Colors of bright laid sparkles on the enchanted forest meadow
The sun shone through with streaks of white rays

You could hear the whistling wind playing tunes from a violin
Streams of water frozen by the wintry air
Rocks cuddled in the bed of the frozen streams
Leaves of moisture gave warmth to the forest meadow floor

Beauty in time spent under the colorful blanket of nature

END OF THE DAY

The awakening morning came too soon
While birds played their melody of tunes
Soft rays of light came rushing through
Warming sounds held the morning dew
Stillness of the air brought a new thought through
Love holds light what you hold dear
Joy of knowing a presence is near
The heart is light...the feet are swift moving through the thick of it
Noon became morning as we shuffled on by holding onto the feelings inside
What wondrous things we come to know as the glory of life continuously grows
The hustle and bustle a daily show
Carried out by the two legged people we know
Noon became dusk with our hearts aglow
For serenity is found in all we behold
The quiet ride home I became to know
As the Does stood before me with their heads bent low

Heartfelt Warmth

Frost lay heavy on the carpeted forest floor of white
warming the buds from fall
The deer and does rush in to savor what has not been spoiled
under the Winter Solstice
Like all things that live and breathe
We too rest under the winter heaven
When loss engulfs our being
We rest more nurturing the soul back to life
As the carpeted forest floor melts away its' frost
So does our heart melt away the sadness under the cushioned wall
The heart blossoms by a passerby
Life begins again in knowing you can truly love and be loved
The heart sheds the flakes like drifting snow that falls off the mountain tops
You glide over the universe with beautiful wings of feathery light
Like a condor in full flight, touching all with pleasurable splendor
Giving thanks for all the earthly wonders that encompass our being
Knowing your feelings and words travel the universe under the whispering tongue
You bask under the Sun in pure delight

HEAVEN AND EARTH

When rain falls it caresses the wind
The wind moves it gently through the heavens
It finds a place to rest below the sky
Puddles form creating a rainbow of colors

It gives an unusual sense of peace with sadness
Running with our thoughts
We are able to reach inside our hearts
To embrace the music of the falling drops

Rain, a cleansing of the earth
and our souls
Walk in the silence of the raindrops
Let the body heal from within

Take time to understand why you are here
Know the meaning of life which has been given
Touch the wind
Let it blow gentle circles around your being

Bring joy into your heart
Smile a thousand kisses of raindrops
Let your feet be lifted to carry you on a remarkable journey
Remember how you came to be

LADY OF THE NIGHT

In the stillness of the night, under the silence of the air
The moon was full as it hung from the sky in the shadows of the stars

Triumphantly she dashed in front of me and sleekly, humbly turned
She wanted to be noticed
With her red fur wrapped as an overcoat around her body
Her eyes met the onlooker and she became a statue cloaked in stillness

Still, so very still, the sleek body held the presence of a monarch

Her gaze engulfed my being, our souls met with an understanding of their own
While her tail swept the earthy floor, she swiftly made her way across the lawn

The night was truly worth the ride

LIFE

The light shined dimly upon the Lilly pond
Creeping through the overgrown trees

A frog basked under the sun as he lied on a beautiful Lilly pad
with one leg crossed over his bent leg and his hands
comfortably tucked under the back of his neck

He lay perfectly still listening to the enchanted sounds of the dimly lit forest

Without a care he lay there
The heart beat musically to all that surrounded him

Realizing the sounds of life's creations

The visual brought sweet tunes to the dismal day

MOVEMENT

The rippling sky gave way as the waves rushed through
While the sea carried the sun to distant shores
The land lay barren from the lifeless trees
The wind had nothing to swirl around
Clouds smothered the empty sky
Flocks flew none
Below you saw sands above and mountains low
Empty of all wild life
Hollow were the caves
Sky below and earth above
Changes embraced the galaxy on sand
Movement became truth

Nature In Bloom

Softly touched by the flowering bud through the
early morning openings to sounds in the air
from the flowers dancing in the warm breeze
They blossom knowing that fall will cover them
with a blanket of leaves wet from the early morning dew

Winter brings in the cold
Still the buds are warmed by the fall blanket
The frost adds its' cloak of dripping peaceful snow

All things living under this vast universe
Bask in the love of coming to life again

Spring opens the hearts of the sleepy rows of flowers
Blowing in the breeze on their thinly dressed stems
While the leaves unwrap the joy of the sun
Given birth to them once again

Lie on the untouched bed of blooms
Smell the sweetness of the romantic drizzle
Dream under the sun
While the clouds form a picture of faces old and new
The sky of blue is comforted, given space to all we view

Nature

Looking over your shoulder
You see the world so differently
All is calm and you smile lovingly to the sounds of nature
As the bodies of waters move, the sky engages with them
The clouds join in to a melody of tunes
Then the pitter patter of the falling rain creates its own music
To add to the mix, the raindrops turn to hail
Throwing in another mix of melodies
The thunder comes in like drums, moving the clouds around
The orchestra has been created by the moving melodies of nature
Soothingly, joyfully the sun out shines them all
The sounds are now of violins over the ripples of waters
You are swept off your feet and your toes are dancing
Electrifyingly all has become a tune of colors
The flowers are dancing, the birds are singing
Nature has a wonderful sound
Just listen and enjoy – live and love

SOUNDS OF THE FOREST

Go into the hollow of your soul
Listen while walking through the forest
While the trees blow in the wind
You can hear them singing
The wind carries their tunes throughout the universe
Soft blowing melodies polish the winds
The winds send out sound waves
Only you can hear
Through the branches the sounds become clearer
The rhythm is soothing to the ear
The hollow of the soul cries for more to appear
The turning of the leaves bring in an unusual sound
The birds fly out of their nest as they are being lifted
to the sound of flight
They assure your life is living within the wild
The forest holds your being
The soul has been awakened

SOUNDS

We saw nothing but the Sounds
The darkness held the light
We huddled together and whispered....hushed words
Sounds of fleeting, swishing movements bellowing spats of air
Forming crystalized water surrounded us...our breathing was all we heard...
We moved with the speed of sounds echoing overhead
The forest floor heavy under flight
Behind us the Sounds grew soft
Around us the clouds colored light with movement in sight
Through it all...the night became day
The Sounds...were a mixture of bitter sweet delight
We saw nothing
The Sounds?
Became the mystery of the Night

UNEARTHED OF LIGHT

We listened and heard not the birds calling us
Saw the flowers limp from rain
Tree limbs crushed by the storm
Fallen mountains making their own road

We listened and heard not the call of all
Mystical movements not seen
Mysteriously we silently moved through the towering trees

We listened and heard not the thunder
The clouds were running through the sounds overhead
We shuddered and held ourselves close together

We listened and saw not the rain pouring down
Footed puddles splashed our bodies as we moved

Streams of sunlight opened the sky to colors of blue
We listened and saw not the beauty
Heard the quiet in the earth

UNTAMED

Whispery Ocean Breezes
Wind Swept Sands
Painted Clouds Of Old
Wrapped In Precious Hands

Snow Draped Mountain Tops
Icicles Hanging High and Low
covered in a Blanket of Snow

Rushing Waterfalls
Earth Beaten Trails
Leafless Trees Barren by Winter
Surrounding Your Soul

Skies of Sparkling White
Soft Falling Raindrops

Winter in Summer
Fall in Spring

Untamed Mysteries is what He brings

Winter In Night

Snow covered evergreens showing off their tops
Captured by the looking glass sparkling in the dark
The fresh crisp air filling our lungs with the delicacies of life
While the Coyote's look for their pups in the streams of light
In and out they run through their luxurious den
Only to find their cuddly ones watching at the other end
Bringing sweetness and love throughout the night
Watching the falling snowflakes dazzling our hearts with delight
The charismatic snow covered trees warm with ice
As the watchful prey is always in flight
The Owls that listen with a gourmet's delight
While our four legged and winged friends
look for their meals throughout the night
With the sweet fullness of comfort flowing through them all
Four legged, Winged Tip, Evergreens and more
It comes to past as it came to be
The Beauty of Life lives within Me

WINTER IN WINTER

The ocean floor moved slowly under the crusted cover of the icy white blanket
Covered by the moving waves underneath
Heavy with peaks of creamy white caps forming mountain tops
across the endless bay
Holding the Unicorns in a stream of white frost

The air was sharp and bitter cold creating an elegant winter scene

Trees unable to bend as the branches held their winter ice
where once leaves spurned from them
or flowers had nestled under the warming sun

Stillness hung tight and rapture rang songs of heavenly delight
Snowflakes covered the earthy terrain and formed
colorful rays of sparkling bright
on the drifting icy caps as they floated across the bay coming to life again
Breaking the ice for the Unicorns to move majestically light

Mesmerized by the serene peace winter brings
Stillness was all that was heard

WONDERMENT

You watch as the leaf falls from its' branch
The wind takes it on a breath taking journey
It travels over brooks and streams
Slowly it rests on a Lily pond
Then the wind gushes in again – and off it goes
Moving through the empty space of nowhere
It travels on its' own
You run to see where it will land again
The wind is brisk and takes it high in the air
You lose sight of it
You continue to run through the earthy meadows
Finding peace in movement
The wonderment of how the leaf can be so majestically full of life
You see yourself in flight and the Heavens were as you thought them to be
You glow and the Heavens carried you higher and higher
Gloriously nothing else matters
Effortlessly your body moves like a breath of fresh air
Never to stop floating

About the Poet

Donna Marie (Andrews) Rose was born in Newport, Rhode Island and presently resides in Portsmouth with her Shiloh Shepherd, Da'Naho and her Himalayan cat, Sweetie.

Beholding is Donna's first book of poems, and she is currently working on a novel based on Life, Death and her connection to the Other Side.

Donna is an Office Manager/Supervisor by trade. She is expert in bookkeeping, medical billing and personnel management.

Additionally she is a Certified Caregiver along with teaching Tai Chi, Chi'uan and Meditation.

"For years I felt I had healed as much as the human heart and mind could heal. Writing poetry, I was truly amazed by what prolifically flowed out of my heart and soul on to paper. I discovered my writing is a way of healing myself in a most unusual way. Whenever I write, I listen to beautiful, soft music, and it enhances what comes out of me."

Made in the USA
Columbia, SC
07 May 2018